THE LAST OF THE

Poor Boys

AN EXCITING ADVENTURE IN LIVING 1934–TO ?

To Charlotte & Steve
Be all you can be

Micky Graham

MICKY GRAHAM

"Coal Camp Boy"
A West "By God" Virginian
Mountaineers are always free!

NEWMAN SPRINGS PUBLISHING
320 Broad Street
Red Bank, NJ 07701

First originally published by Newman Springs Publishing 2020

ISBN 978-1-64801-180-1 (Paperback)
ISBN 978-1-64801-181-8 (Digital)

Printed in the United States of America

To my family. Without them, I could not have achieved my goals and dreams.

To my parents, grandparents, wives, and relatives who supported me in all my endeavors. My son and grandchildren who have made me proud and happy.

Margy, Alan and Micky Graham

Grandchildren—Laura, Zachary, Wesley

My son Alan, grandchildren, Wesley, Zachary, and Laura are all self-motivated.

The *fire in the belly* has moved on to the second and third generation intact.

No parent and grandparent could ask for more. *Mission accomplished.*

CONTENTS

Special recognition to Randy Doell, CPC

PREFACE

What I hope to accomplish with this history of my life.

Life is a continuous journey from launchpad to even better life. Finding your individual plan of life and setting goals in ways to achieve the joy in life.

First, we must realize very young that we come from some place, and we are on an exciting trip called life. Finding one's purpose and direction is the miracle of life. We must begin as a poor boy or girl to appreciate this miracle.

Humility must be with you forever, or as my mother would say, don't get to "big for your britches." Hard work is the driving force of life. No one or the government owes you anything. Our rights as Americans are defined in the Constitution and Bill of Rights. Everything else in life is a privilege that must be earned.

Making good choices based on good sound values is a must for the transition to being a rich boy or girl.

A good sense of humor is the energy and grease to get through the tough times of life. Laughing is good medicine. You must learn to laugh at yourself as well as others. The people I remember in my journey as a poor boy either made me laugh or set a good example. It made me think. Everyone else fell into one big "I can't remember."

It is my hope that this book will motivate young people to be rich, not necessarily in financial terms but rich in life.

Napoleon Hill said it best in *Think and Grow Rich*. I would add happiness and fulfillment each all boils down to this. In order to make a poor boy into a rich boy, you must understand the MISS or MRS theory and turn it into S—success. The theory works this way to achieve financial independence.

M = Marry it
I = Inherited
S = Steal it
S = Save it

The only one that works is the last S. Save it and let it grow. If you do not do any of the preceding four, you will have your MRS degree.

M = Miserable
R = Rotten
S = Struggle

The MISS-MRS in the strictest sense applies to women.
For poor boys or girls, the WIN will work every time this is.

W = What's
I = Important
N = Now

And in conclusion, remember this bedrock quote for life: "If it is to be, it is up to me." Go for it!

INTRODUCTION

by Randy Doell, a longtime friend

_ _ _ _ _

CHAPTER 1

"Meeting" House Branch before WWII

I was born on October 7, 1934. The place was Meeting House Branch. It was up a "holler" between Baileysville and Clear Fork, West Virginia. It was in the middle of the Great Depression. We lived on my grandparents' hillside farm. My father could not find work. Times were very hard. There was no doctor to deliver my mother—miles from the nearest hard-topped road, no electricity, inside plumbing, water, or telephone. The house was a clapboard two-room built by my father. I was named Alfred L. Graham, Jr. after my father. He nicknamed me Micky the same day. That's another story.

Welfare, food stamps, unemployment compensation, heath care, and the hundreds of government programs did not exist. People depended on themselves and family. It was a great time to become a poor boy. *My family would not have taken charity.*

My grandparents were hardworking people and never owned a car or traveled over fifty miles from home. How they raised five children was indeed a miracle. Everyone was taught to work; hoeing corn and doing chores at the age of six was expected. My grandfather was an ordained minister with only a second-grade education. He read his Bible every day and practiced what he preached. My grandmother was barely five feet tall and weighed maybe a hundred pounds. But look out! She was the boss and made my grandfather at a hundred and ninety pounds do what she said. He loved it. He told me before I married to find a good woman and let her be the boss. It worked for him, and he was happy always and only saw the good in people. He was always positive, and it had a great influence on my life. So did my grandmother. And I never knew my grandparents on my mother's side because they had died.

Before we get into the adventures and misadventures of life, a reflection on my parents. My mother was a redhead in-charge woman with an English and Irish ancestry. My father was tall, had jet black hair and an ancestry of Scottish and Cherokee Indian.

With this background, for a life of humor, I was destined for life with a little mischief and mayhem thrown into the pot.

The early days on Meeting House Branch were filled as many unforgettable experience. Looking back on life, now going on at eighty-five years, I remembered mostly happy positive events with a zest for life and adventure. Throughout out this journey of life, I will name "turning points" that shaped my character, directions, and goals.

Life was fun in the late thirties, even though times were hard and we were poor. So was everyone else so I didn't know I was a poor boy until I moved to Ohio twenty-five years later in 1959. To Ohioans, West Virginians were dumb hillbillies. *It was fun to realize I had more motivation than they did.*

I enjoyed going into the woods, climbing trees, turning over rocks, looking for crawfish, rolling barrel hoops with a piece of wire fence formed into a hook, going after the cows for milking, and catching June bugs and many more outdoor activities.

My cousins, brother and sister, Jack and Jill Cook lived at the mouth of Meeting House Branch about a half mile away.

My Aunt Allie and Uncle Curtis's home was my second home. We walked everywhere as no one had a car until later. There were two churches at Elk Lick now called Clearfork, West

Virginia. One was my grandparents' Advent Christian church, and the other was a holiness church. We called them *holy rollers*. And they did. As kids, we would walk through pastures and woods to spy on them and listen to the shouting, dancing, stomping, and singing. To us kids, it was entertaining.

We amused ourselves by playacting what we would witness at church. We had big imaginations. One day the three of us decided to play church—that is, Jack and Jill and myself. I preached, Jill sang, and Jack took up a collection. All three of us shouted and testified. After a while, we decided to have a baptism service. There was a rain barrel at the barn. The cats had kittens, and they were the first to be baptized. Next was the mother cat. She did not like it, but we were determined and finally put her under. The old tomcat stayed in the barn and was hard to catch. Jack finally caught him, and we headed to the rain barrel. "Old tom" wanted no part of the baptism. He reacted as tomcats do with hisses and claws. He dug into Jack's arm, causing him to bleed. With that, Jack drops old tom and says, "Let's just sprinkle him and let him *go to hell.*" With that, old Tom headed for the high country. So much for baptisms. I found out later that Methodists sprinkle. Jack must have been a Methodist.

West Virginia mountain humor kept us together in hard times. Sitting on the front porch before dusk and exchanging stories by our grandparents, uncles, and aunts was the happiness that prepared us for bed. There was no Dr. Phil, Oprah, psychotherapy doctors, counselors, or social workers, just a good family. We did not need any of them.

One story my dad told which became more hilarious as I become an adult was the story of "Hicks Massie" and his conversions at the Holiness Church. Hicks and his wife "Thulie" got saved about every time the church had a revival. It seems that after the preacher had preached a "hellfire and brimstone" sermon, Hicks would go forward again. He then would share his testimony. He and Thulie had several children. Hicks was going to live for the Lord and so was his family. He was a little "tongue-tied" now, called a speech impediment. He ended his long testimony with the classic statement: "Me and Thulie and the kids are going to live for the Lord, or I will beat the godda—hell out of all of them." He had become a man of conviction, at least until the next revival.

TURNING POINT
LAUGH HARD, LAUGH OFTEN, AND IT
WILL STAY WITH YOU FOREVER

Those early years on "Meeting House Branch" were happy ones. We were indeed poor but didn't know we were. We were rich in spirit, family, and love for one another.

My grandparent's farm consisted of sixty-seven acres, mostly wooded and mountainous. Yellow Tulip Popular trees were plentiful. My dad built a log cabin for us out of logs he cut from the straight trees. This was about 1938 to 1939. It consisted of four rooms—a big step from two rooms. My sister was born there in 1941. The bathtub hung on a nail outside the back door. A wood-and-coal burning "burnside" stove heated the cabin. It was either too hot or too cold. The nearest water was a mountain spring about a hundred yards away. My mother told me that she would tie me to the bedstead by the ankle while she went to get a bucket of water. I was a toddler at the time and into everything.

My grandmother had made me two "feed-sack" diapers. One was on me and the other was on the clothesline. Back then, feed and grain for the animals were bought in feed sacks. They were usually of a flower or print design. Nothing went to waste. Shirts, dresses, diapers, etc. were made out of all the empty feed sacks.

No one complained about the economy. Everyone worked their gardens, crops, ginseng, dug up Mayapple roots, and traded "butter and eggs" for basics at the store three miles away. Yes, we were like the Little House on the Prairie, only we called it the cabin up the creek.

My dad finally got a real job about 1938. The railroad was coming through for all the coal mines that were opening. He worked as a laborer from 6:00a.m. to 6:00p.m for $2.00 a day. It was big money at the time. It would buy a lot of pinto beans, salt, and sugar. He walked seven miles to work through the mountains. He left well before daylight and got home usually after dark. Later on, about 1940, he got a job as a meat cutter for the A.M. Harris store in Gary, West Virginia, McDowell County. The coal mines and World War II had brought economic revival to the mountains. Since he did not have a car, he boarded in Gary, which was about thirty to thirty-five miles away. He would borrow the store truck a 1939 International pickup every two or three weeks. I learned to drive by sitting on a Pepsi wood crate at about nine years old in that old truck.

It wouldn't be long before we started our many moves. Our first move was only about one mile to a real house that had a well. But before we move, I must tell the story of my grandfather and the drunk on a horse. It was not unusual during the '30s for someone to ride up on a horse. I do not know who he was, but my grandfather knew him. He rode up to where my grandfather was chopping wood for the stove and I was stacking it for him. I must have been about four years old.

He was obviously very drunk and swearing and loud. My grandfather who was very strict said he didn't allow cursing in front of his grandchildren. At that point, the drunk said godda— your grandchildren. That was the last thing he said as my grandfather (I called him pa) jumped up in the air and hit the drunk so hard it knocked him out cold with one punch. He picked up the drunk and draped him across the saddle and slapped the horse to go. The horse went about thirty feet to the creek, and he slid off into the creek. My grandfather pulled him up and took him to the house, sobered him up, and kept him all night.

The next day as he was leaving a humbled man, my grandfather told him, "You are welcome to come back, but I do not allow cursing in front of my grandchildren."

The man responded, "Uncle Floyd, I will never cuss in front of your grandchildren again." And he didn't. "Pa"/"Uncle Floyd" had made his point. Pa was a very strong man about 5"9" or 5"10 and weighed between 185-190 pounds. He was a man with a round chest, a hardworking farmer and laborer.

Turning Point
Make a Stand and Don't Run from a Problem

Stand up for what you believe but love your fellow man. That was my grandfather. He didn't take any "lip" but would help anyone or even give away most anything he had.

My grandmother, "Ma," barely five feet tall, was in charge of Pa and let him know it. She was strong-willed, opinionated, and hardworking. She worked her big garden, canned, cured, picked berries, milked the cows, fed the hogs, raised her chickens, and grew beautiful flowers. She cooked three meals a day on her wood-and-coal stove. We had fresh biscuits or cornbread for every meal. My favorite meal today is soup beans, cornbread, and buttermilk.

She churned her own butter, and there was always fresh milk. Her refrigerator was the cellar dug into the hill. The only hot water was heated on the stove or the tank on the side of the stove that kept it warm. One wash pan and feed sack towel was on the back porch. No one seemed to get sick or have health problems. Think of the germs we shared.

She made the best fried apple pies in her cast iron skillet. She would make a stack of them, sprinkle powdered sugar on top, and set them in the warming oven on the old stove. That was our desert our treats. She cooked on that old stove for most of her life as she was married in 1901 at age fourteen and died in 1961. They were married sixty years. And as "Pa" said, marry a good woman and let her be the boss, and so she was. My grandfather worked two years for my great-grandfather. My great-great-grandfather gave him a choice of his daughters as payment. He chose *Roxie*; she was a good choice.

Electricity came up the creek in 1946. This changed everything.

They could stay up later, have a radio to listen to Lum & Abner, Amos & Andy, Lowell Thomas, and the Grand Ole Oprey. Life was good.

In 1951, I started getting paid working at the coal company store. Between my dad and I, we bought her an electric stove. Sometime later, we were visiting and saw that the electric stove was not being used. As Ma explained, it wouldn't bake bread like the coal stove. So much for progress.

I bought them their first television set about 1953. There was only one station WSAZ in Huntington West Virginia. To get reception, an antenna had to be installed on top of the mountain and wire run to the house. I did this, and they were overjoyed. Ma loved Saturday night "rasslin." She thought it was real. She was a religious God-fearing woman, but she would get excited when the bad guys on "rasslin" would hurt the good guy. She would clinch her fist and say, "Look at the *Sum Bitch.*" Imagine cursing in front of her grandchildren. *Sum Bitch* was her word when she got mad at the cows, chickens, or some person. It was time to get out of the way.

She was also a practical joker. She invented a fictional character *"Ole Dick"* to scare us grandchildren. Ole Dick consisted of her under a blanket quilt making terrible noises and chasing us. She would catch us by surprise playing in the yard. Of course, we ran and screamed. One day remembering my grandfather's example, I thought that *"Ole Dick"* had hurt my grandmother. I grabbed the double bit axe from the wood pile and ran toward "Ole Dick" under the blanket, yelling, "I'm coming, Ma! I will kill the *son-of-a-bitch.*" *"Ole Dick"* quickly shed the quilt and was rolling on the ground with laughter.

I had put an end to "Ole Dick," and I had also learned my first cuss word and unfortunately have used it over the years to describe the worthlessness of society.

During the '30s the Depression was on to World War II. Times were hard, and men we called tramps or hobos came around all the time. My grandfather had a habit to bring them home unannounced for a meal. Ma had to do the work, and food was hard to get. One day Pa brought this man home that stunk like "B.O. Plenty." He was dirty and had hair over his ears. After she had fed him, and he was on his way, Ma promptly got the loaded shotgun behind the bedroom door. She marched out on the front porch and made her testimony with the barrel under my Pa's chin. She said, "Floyd Graham, if you ever bring a dirty *Sum Bitch* for me to cook for again, I will blow you head off." He never did again.

TURNING POINT
THERE IS A LIMIT TO EVERYTHING

I have memories of being a happy kid who spent a lot of time in the woods, creeks, fields, and surrounding farms. As all boys of that time, mischief and mayhem played a part of growing up.

One summer night, my cousins and I decided we would steal a watermelon from one of my cousin's dad's patch. We had our own watermelon patch, but a stolen one would taste better. It was the Belcher place, and two of the Belcher boys were in on the heist. As we were heading to the fence with our watermelons, someone tripped over a line filled with tin cans and bells.

This was the alarm someone or something was in the garden. We had to crawl under the barbed wire fence to get out. It was pitch black and there was no moon. As I was going under the fence on my belly, I panicked and came up too fast, burying the barbed wire in the rear pockets of my overalls. The barbed wire not only tore my "overalls" but what they were covering. The watermelon had lost its taste, and I had to explain what happened to my pants to my mother. She added insult to injury by applying psychology over the same torn overalls. Another limb off the willow tree.

Turning Point
Never Take Anything that Is Not Yours
I Never Did Again

I started school in 1939 at the age of five as my mother helped at the school, and I had to go with her. It was at Laurel Branch about two miles away through the fields. It was on a hill with a good view of the dirt road below. It had been a two-room school, now a one-room with all eight grades. At any given time, there were twenty-five to thirty students ranging in age from six to twenty to twenty-one or so. The restrooms were air-conditioned down a path behind the school. Both the girls and boys had two seats so there was no waiting. An occasional black snake would make its home in one, and when you heard a scream from the girls' toilet, you knew. Life was good.

Of course, no boy at that age would dare catch a blacksnake and hide it the girls' toilet—certainly not me.

Discipline was strict and quick. There were no parent teacher conferences, no phone calls to home or detention halls. Discipline consisted of three forms: (1) Go stand in the corner, (2) put your nose in a circle on the blackboard, (3) and over the desk for the board of education.

A sad memory of the times occurred at the school. One of the girls from Laurel Branch took my paper bag lunch and ran to the girls' toilet. Her name was Dorothy and she came from a poorer family than mine and obviously, she was hungry.

Turning Point
There Will Always Be Someone that Has Less
than You Never Turn Down a Hungry Person

It was at Laurel Branch School that I met Miss Donna Jean Harvey, the new teacher. She was the daughter of a neighbor who owned a store near the school. I was in the second or third grade at the time. One day she asked me to stay after school. Much to my surprise, she was not giving me a lecture or a note to take home. Instead she told me I should go to college someday. I didn't know what "college" was. That idea stuck in my mind. From that day on, I dreamed of going to college. No one in my family had ever graduated from high school.

My grandparents had two or three years of school at the most. My dad went to the eleventh grade and my mother to the eighth grade. Both had to drop out to go to work.

Using one's imagination was fun and entertaining. In the summer, the "June bugs" were everywhere. They were flying green beetle-type bugs about the size of a large kidney bean up to a big one, the size of your little toe. We would catch them and tie a string around one of their legs and let it fly around the yard. Our imagination led us to tying two June bugs, one on each end of the string about six feet long.

That was fun as they would pull different ways with us holding the string with one hand in the middle. One day one of the laying hens spotted one of the June bugs and caught it in midair. *It was off to egg country.* The other June bug with the remaining string was flying with the old hen trying to catch it. Down the path went the June bug with string coming out of the chicken's beak. A funny sight as I yelled to Ma that a June bug was stealing one of her chickens.

The June bugs had several legs. When you would catch one and hold it in your hands, it would crawl and tickle you as it did. Someone, *not me*, got the idea that maybe one tied under the cat's tail would provide some massage therapy to a lazy cat. Using a small piece of thread, the cat was outfitted with this special June bug. Seems as if under the cat's tail was the ideal place to conduct the experiment.

Needless to say, the cat went into overdrive, not forward but round and round trying to get at what was tickling her funny bone. If only that energy could have been used for catching mice. The fun was short lived as my mother saw what was happening and promptly tickled my "funny bone." Another limb off the willow tree.

Each summer, I would spend time with two other first cousins, Billy and Dennie Graham. Billy was as ornery as I was, if not more. His mother said that I was the orneriest boy she ever saw. Then along came Billy. She retracted her statement. An example of his mischief is as follows.

I was about fourteen at the time and tall for my age. I was to spend a week with my Uncle Herbert and Aunt Kat, the parents of Billy. They lived in Glen Rogers, West Virginia, another coal camp.

Billy had told all the coal camp boys I was coming for a visit. He had told them I was a champion Golden Gloves boxer. Guess what, three of them wanted to find out by jumping me at the same time. Luckily for me, it was on the road up a steep embankment to Billy's house. Billy was hiding in the distance, full of laughter.

I did not give the first one a chance. Catching him off guard, one punch sent him rolling down the embankment. The second boy was next. I tripped him up, and over the embankment he went. The third one ran down the hill.

Billy thought it was funny, but he would have been there with me if it came to that. I can truly say I am related to Billy Graham—not the preacher but the barber. He operates a barber shop in Oak Hill West Virginia called Billy Graham's Hair Revival. We are brothers more than cousins. We take care of each other.

One of my chores living on my grandparent's farm was to round up the cows for milking. "Porky" the dog and I would go up the hill to find them usually in the woods. Porky did most of the work rounding them up at the barn. For his efforts, he quickly got some fresh milk.

My grandmother had a milking stall with a feed box. The cows would be tied at the halter to the post above the feed box. One cow, Ole Red, never wanted to stand still during milking. She would often step right into the milk bucket, a two-gallon galvanized water bucket. This upset my fiery grandmother who often called Ole Red a "*Sum Bitch.*" One day in particular, Ole Red was swatting flies with her tail and hit my grandmother in the face several times, and again, Ole Red stepped in the milk bucket. Ma had enough. She decided if she put a weight on the cow's tail, so she couldn't swing it. She proceeded to tie a short rope connected to part of a cinder block on the ground. That didn't faze Ole Red. Round came the tail with the cinder block, hitting my grandmother on the side of her head, broke her glasses, and cut her face. Ma's fiery temper got the best of her. She headed up to the woodpile and got a large piece of white oak and swung it several times between the horns of Ole Red. Sum Bitch was used again in front of her grandchild. Ole Red must have gotten the message as she was a lot easier to milk after that.

Milking time was a special time. Both the cat and dog were there for a treat. The dog had a pan to lap up the milk. The cat would catch the milk as Ma would squirt it in the cat's face. It was a ritual twice a day. The cat and the dog got along. Each knew their place.

Ma and Pa raised chickens, so we always had fresh eggs. I enjoyed going to the henhouse and collecting the eggs out of the nest. Occasionally, at night, foxes and coons and sometimes stray dogs would raid the henhouse. If the door was left open, hawks were always a threat to chickens in the open. That's why there was always a loaded shotgun behind the door.

During the day, sometimes a blacksnake would invade the henhouse. They liked eggs or baby chicks. The hoe was always nearby for a quick execution.

Old chickens eventually ended up in the pot or frying pan. Chicken and dumplings were one of my favorite meals. Eventually, I was given the job of preparing a chicken for the table. This was not pleasant. The ax and chopping block were used. It was not a pretty sight, but someone had to do it. Perhaps the worst of it was removing the feathers in scalding hot water. Plucking the chicken as it called will stay with you forever. I did not eat chicken again for many years.

Beans, "taters," and cornbread were fine with me. If anyone could smell the odor of plucking a chicken or see a chicken run after losing its head, there would be a lot less "*eat more chicken.*"

I had trouble eating squirrels. Squirrel gravy and biscuits was a mainstay. There were few rabbits as foxes and dogs kept the population limited.

At Thanksgiving time, Pa would kill a hog, and neighbors would help for a *mess* of fresh meat. This was my first experience as a meat cutter. My father was a butcher by trade and taught me how to dress a cow, hog, or deer. Later over at the coal mine store, I became the butcher. Many of the miners called you "Butch."

Killing a hog required boiling water, sharp knives, a "spreader," and a cold day. The meat was canned, smoked, or "salt-cured." The hams were smoked or sometimes cured with salt in the smokehouse. The table in the smokehouse was used to place the fatback bacon shoulders, etc. The salt preserved the meat. My grandmother would go cut off slices of salt bacon to fix. She rolled it in meal. It was good. They made sausage and "cold packed" it in canning jars.

Nothings better on a cold winter morning than hot biscuits and gravy.

The food was great but consisted of a lot of potatoes, pinto beans, vegetables out of the garden and creasy greens out of the yard in the spring. Fresh cornbread crumbled in a glass of buttermilk was dessert at the end of supper on the front porch about dark listening to the "Whippoorwills." It was a special time.

I would miss that simple lifestyle. Looking back, those early days up the "holler" surrounded by the mountains were filled with contentment. *I have never lived anywhere that gave me that same feeling.*

World War II came as shock. Everyone rallied around our country. The great generation had begun. My uncle Willard joined the army. He later served with Patton's third army and went through the battle of the bulge. He had several medals including the Silver Star. My uncle Charlie Hurst had joined the army in 1937 and earned a commission. He retired as a full bird colonel. He only had an eighth grade education. He later worked at the Oak Ridge Atomic Bomb Plant in Tennessee. He was either CIA or Secret Service. We found out later after his death, he was a GS-16, equivalent to a four-star general. He was also a pilot. His wife never knew what he was doing or where he was when away on a mission. My cousin, O.J. Gill, a veteran of World War II, Korea, and Vietnam found this information when he was assigned to Pentagon duty. O.J. retired as a Lt. Colonel in the army. Several of my cousins served in the army or air force. Two served for twenty years.

I was the odd ball. I joined the Marine Corps and had the great honor of serving under Hershel "Woody" Williams who held the Congressional Medal of Honor from Iwo Jima. He was a role model for me. He was far different from most Marine Sergeants. He was quiet, humble, and you respected him immediately. I was honored to stand formation with him as he was made a commissioned warrant officer by President Eisenhower in 1958. I have a copy of his medal of honor and an autographed copy of Iwo Jima. We were both West Virginians, and proud of it.

To this day it bothers me when people say to you, "Are you from Virginia or Western Virginia?" We mountaineers have a clarification for the world. It is "No, we are from West 'By God' Virginia." Mountaineers are always free men. Two other ancestors should be mentioned in my small contribution to history. One was my great-grandfather Graham who fought in the Civil War for the confederacy. The other was on my mother's side, Mary Inglies. The book and movie *Follow the River* was the story of her capture and escape from the Indians.

My family has a history of speaking their minds. Before they fled Scotland, they feuded with the king, and some of them were hung.

My father, grandfather, and uncles were all men who knew what they believed and were not afraid to say it. This Graham trait in my life would sometimes cause me to bear the consequences. I wouldn't change a thing. I have no problem looking in the mirror. Enough of this beginning, it's time to go the next journey of joy.

My grandfather several times removed on my mother's side was Jacob Albert, who was a scout or spy for George Washington in the revolutionary war.

After returning to his home in West Virginia, he could never walk without crutches. He nearly froze at Valley Forge with George Washington.

He became a peddler, taking his wagon and horses to Roanoke, Virginia to bring supplies into the mountains. He brought the first coffee beans into now Southern West Virginia. No one knew what coffee beans were. He sold some of them. When he returned to his coffee bean customers the next trip, a disgruntled mountaineer informed him that his wife had cooked the coffee beans with salt back for three hours, and they still tasted bad.

He lived to ninety-nine and supported his family on crutches without Uncle Sugar to do it for him. Proud of my ancestors. Good role models.

CHAPTER 2

Learning the Work Ethic

World War II brought an end to the depression. The coal mines were starting everywhere in southern West Virginia. Mining grew from its start in the '20s and '30s to its hay day in the '40s. In the future, things began to slow down, and the unionized mines went the way that the auto makers are today. *The lesson I learned early in life is when the tail wags the dog, the dog will lose its bite.*

We left the holler for McDowell County. We lived in an apartment in Welch on the second floor. This was not for me. No creeks, trees, cows, or dogs. It was noisy and cramped. My dad worked at the A.N. Harris store in Gary. It was not long until we moved back to the Clear Fork area of West Virginia. I was happy to be back with my grandparents, family, and the woods.

I could fish and swim in the river and shoot squirrels. At age ten, I could shoot a rifle and shotgun. My father taught me to safely handle guns. I never forgot it. I did just what he told me. All boys where I grew up learned this life lesson.

Many of the young men were leaving for the military. Most volunteered and the draft took the rest except those that got deferred or could not pass the physical. Some had political strings pulled to keep them out.

TURNING POINT
"DRAFT DODGERS" HAD NO RESPECT
FROM ANYONE I KNEW

My uncle was in the Army. My dad was ready to go, but they were not taking anyone over thirty-five with children. Respect for the military was learned at the young age of eight. Many of my father's and mother's family served in the army, navy, and air force.

I was the only one who chose the Marines—good choice. They took me even though it says, "We are looking for a few good men." I am sure some of my family would question how "good" I was. But thanks to the willow switch, belt, paddle, wooden spoon, or whatever, I made it.

Next was a move from the country to the coal camps. Coal camps at that time were booming, and one could find work, live in a coal company house, have a coal company store, and live in a community with a common lifestyle. This was my introduction to inside plumbing, electricity, and all the luxuries I had heard about.

My father was a butcher who ran the meat and produce department. He would later become the store manager. During World War II, many things were rationed. There were meat points, coupons, etc.

This was fine with me as I had learned to live on beans and "taters" and the garden. My favorite meal still today is soup beans and fresh cornbread—pinto beans, that is. Parlay that with a glass of churned buttermilk, we would crumble the cornbread into the buttermilk and eat it with a spoon. I learned to add salt and pepper and yes, mustard. Still eat it that way today.

There were no allowances for kids back then as it took everything for food, clothing, and the necessities of life. We were taught to take care of what we had and make it last as long as possible, which brings me to another turning point.

Turning Point
Take Care of What You Have
and Make the Most of It

I remember wearing my school shoes out in the summer and showing them off to the other boys. All boys went barefoot in the summer and saved their shoes for school. And yes, sometimes you cut the toes out as you grew or wore hand-me-downs. It was a hot day, and my pals went to the creek to play. I had my school shoes on in the water, kicking rocks. My mother caught me. Another limb off the willow tree and all the way home on my bare legs, she said, "I'll teach you to not wear your school shoes in the creek." I never forgot it. Thanks to her, I learned not to waste and conserve what I had. There was no money for frills like two pairs of shoes, designer jeans, etc.

The work ethic began to set in with me. If I wanted something besides the basics, I had to work for it. I hoed corn, mowed yards with a sickle, and push reel mower (no power mowers back then).

My first sales job was at age eight, selling the *Grit*, newspaper for three cents, and I got a penny. I often made twenty-five cents and walked from three to five miles to do it. Later on in the coal camps, I delivered the Charleston Daily mail paper and made a little more money. But if they didn't pay me, I had to pay for their paper, which brought me to another turning point.

Turning Point
Be Careful of Loaning Money Know
Who You Are Dealing With If You Borrow or
Promise to Do Something, Follow Through—
Respect Others and Their Property

At about the age of ten, my dad let me work in the company store. This was a big thing as no other boy could do that. I took the trash out to be burned and swept up, took the ashes out of the coal furnace, put up the pop bottles, and anything else that required a strong back and weak mind.

The store manager let me have a bottle of pop and a candy bar. I was in hog heaven. I did this at eight different company stores by the time I was eighteen. I learned how to butcher from my dad when I became sixteen. I could now be legally put on the payroll. At that time, 1950, we had moved again, and my dad was now the assistant store manager and ran the meat department. Mr. Gibson, the store manager, got the most out of everyone.

I had to interview with several other boys for the job. There was nothing else a sixteen-year-old could do to get a job. The nearest town was several miles away. There was a lot of competition to work in the company store. In my interview, I went to the manager's office and stood before his desk. He had the only seat. After about a minute of questions, he handed me an empty coke bottle and told me to put it on the floor in front door of the store. I immediately took the bottle and ran to the door and put it exactly where he said. I quickly retuned and asked what else he wanted me to do.

Without smiling or showing any emotion, he said, "You're hired." *You do what you are told without asking any questions.*

Turning Point
Everyone Has a Boss—Do What You Are Told and Make It Your Goal to Be the Best

I never forgot it and carried it out in my life. I worked all through high school at this store. My father was the assistant manager, and he was harder than Mr. Gibson to please. It worked out as my father was promoted to manager in another store where my mother worked, and I was given my father's job. At age seventeen, this was unheard of at that time.

I had to give up playing sports in school. It was well worth it to learn the work ethic early in life.

During this time, we lived in six different coal camps, living in company-owned houses. Another big lesson I learned during this time period was that with work comes responsibilities.

My first month on the payroll, I worked all day on Saturday and after school Monday through Friday. I finally got my fist pay about $90.00 for one month. I was excited, and at supper time I was telling my mother, father, and sister what I was going to do with my money. Of course, I was going to save to buy a car.

My dad, without looking up, said to me, "You are a man now it's time to start acting like one. Your room and board will be $60.00." I was stunned and mad, but it didn't matter. I paid it and did so until I left home at age nineteen. They needed the money.

TURNING POINT
YOU HAVE TO PAY YOUR WAY—
NO ONE OWES YOU ANYTHING

The last thing my parents would have done was to accept welfare, food stamps, unemployment compensation, or any government handout. Yes, they were Republican conservatives living in a democrat united mine workers union coal camp. My dad said one time there were only six republicans to every five hundred in our whole camp.

That didn't matter to him; he was who he was. He was a man of conviction.

One of his favorite expressions was "I will pick sh—with the chickens before I change what I believe." It was hard for him to understand when I decided to go to college. I will never forget him saying, "It took me twenty years to get where I am now. You are at it now at nineteen." He never lived to see me graduate. He died in my junior year at age forty-nine. After graduating from college and teaching school for $300 a month, I did think about what he said. Before he died, he was glad I was in college. He knew the coal camps were dying.

I was making more money at the company store. There was still time for girls, activities, school, and cars. I realized that getting married out of high school was not for me. I wanted an education and dreamed of a better life.

Girls still occupied my thoughts and back then girls were taught to be young ladies and you had better be a gentleman if you didn't want her father to come looking for you.

My first car date was with a girl living in the same coal camp. She had never been on a car date either. My dad let me have the car to pick her up. We were going to a school dance. I parked across the railroad tracks and walked to the front door. She met me and invited me in.

Her father was a big rough coal miner. He was sitting in his overstuffed chair. He was at least 6"2 and between 250 and 300 pounds. The hair on his arms and neck looked like they had been planted there. He looked like a big gorilla. He never got out of his chair or shook hands with me. He said, "Boy, I know where you live. You will have her home at 10:00p.m., and I will be watching your every move."

She was as scared as I was. I had her home before 10:00p.m. Teenage pregnancy was unheard of or it was hushed up or concealed. *Lessons learned: respect women or it may be hazardous to your health.* I learned that having sex before marriage was wrong, from my parents and grandparents. It's good to be reminded in a forceful way. I never had a daughter, but if I had, I would have felt the same way. Some boy would have to answer to this old US Marine.

There were many different girlfriends during this time with only two lasting six months or longer. I had a crush on two or three. With the first one, we moved away but married her fifty-two years later. My wonderful first wife had died, and we met by accident. More about that later. Back to the coal camp.

There have been many songs like Tennessee Ernie's "16 tons" and Loretta Lynn's "Coal Miner's Daughter." Both portrayed a hard life. I would like to write a song about a good life in the coal camps. There were many good times and memories. I remember both good and the bad. The sound of the siren in the middle of the night meant there was trouble at the mine. Everyone who could would rush up to the coal tipple mine entrance to wait with great anxiety to see if husband, brother, or Dad was safe. Sometimes it was bad news. I remember one blast that killed nine. I knew a couple of them.

TURNING POINT
LIFE IS SHORT AND ENDS WITHOUT WARNING

If miners were injured and could not work, a box would be placed in the store, and people would buy basic food items and put them in the box. The store would add some meat and milk, and I delivered it to the home along with my regular deliveries.

Very few owned cars, you either carried your groceries home or the store delivered them. The store also sold furniture and appliances, and hundred-pound bags of feed for cows or hogs. I learned to deliver all these items without help. Try putting a hundred-pound bag of feed over your shoulder and carrying a box sometimes up a grade with a dog nipping at your heels. I became very strong with this daily exercise. I was 5"10 and weighed about 130 pounds. I could smash the metal pop and beer bottle caps between two fingers. Still can. They are lighter today on beer bottles, and the pop bottle is almost history.

Neighbor looked after neighbor. There were no secrets in the coal camps. Everyone knew everyone's business. The mine superintendent and the store manager were the only source of authority. In my experience, most were kind, accommodating people. If you worked hard, they took care of you. *It was an honor to work hard.* At a funeral or wake, you would often hear a widow being told your husband was a good worker. There was a great pride in work.

Miners are like every other group of working laborers; some are kind and gentle, and others are rough and tough. I knew both kinds. Mines were often shut down by wildcat strikes. No reason given usually. On the first day of squirrel and deer season, you can almost count on it. The UMW under John L. Lewis had a lot of power and exercised it. I have seen a flatbed truck from some other coal camp pull into the tipple with a load of men with clubs and guns and shut the mine down. No one dared to cross the picket line. There was nothing worse than a scab (one that crosses the picket line).

The company store usually remained open, so for many of them, my dad and I were scabs. Parents would instill this hated word into their children who would challenge someone their own age, like me. If you did not learn to fight, they would pick on you every day. Not all of them were like that, but you could tell who came from the radical UMW homes.

I had my share of fights and met them head on and never ran from anyone or went home crying to mommy and daddy. That would have been humiliating, although I did have to explain why my pants or shirt were torn or soiled. One time in particular, I was just going home from work on Saturday. Store closed early on that day. A friend of my dad drove up and was talking to me. Three miners from a nearby gas station saw him and proceeded to call him a "G.D." scab. He was a security guard at the mines. They knocked him down under his truck and preceded to kick him. I joined in the fight, and they turned on me.

I was all of 130 pounds against three surly men. I was eighteen at the time. Things look bad. I heard this loud voice of my mother: "Leave that boy alone." She had a baseball bat and was trying to crack heads. The miners stopped in their tracks. They respected my mother. "We are sorry, Mrs. Graham," and with that they backed off. I knew as a kid, my mother meant business. They knew you didn't give any lip to big John or my mother.

I had my mother's curly hair which caused the boys to pick on me because the girls liked it. I had a lot of fights over it. When I heard Johnny Cash sing, "My name is Sue," I understood perfectly. Outside of an occasional black eye and two broken noses, it made me a strong, motivated, self-confident young man. You might have figured it out why I joined the Marine Corp.

Mr. William Gibson, or Mr. Bill as he was called, influenced my life. He expected 110 percent from you and got it. He had no children but took me under his wing. He taught me how to work and put yourself into it.

That sadly is missing today with a lot of parents doing *the minimum, not the maximum.* Many children are not given work and responsibility at a young age. It shows with all the video games, cellphones, blackberries, iPads, etc., and are still bored with nothing to do. I always had plenty to do; my parents would invent work for my benefit. I wouldn't have dared to tell them I was bored. I would not have been bored for long.

When my father died in 1957, my mother who had worked in the company store was given his job. She was the only female store manager to my knowledge anywhere during that time. More about this later, I promise it will be interesting.

Working at the company store was hard work. I did everything from firing the coal furnace, taking out the ashes, sweeping, mopping, stocking shelves, and making deliveries to the houses in the coal camp. The store was truly a general store. Everything from dry groceries, meats, produce, clothing, supplies for the miners, tools, hardware, and furniture. At that time 1946-1964, not many miners owned cars. If they did, most wives did not drive. Almost everything was delivered to their homes by me in the company truck. The truck was a 1947 Chevrolet 1.5 ton flat bed with a stake body. The only help I had on large items like washing machines and refrigerators was a dolly. It was a two-wheel pushcart with straps to secure the item being pulled. Mr. Gibson taught me to use leverage and handle it by myself. It was great exercise and I developed strong arms and legs. This brings me to another turning point.

Turning Point
Learn to Do the Hard Jobs by
Yourself, You Can Do It

I delivered washing machines, "wringer type," and refrigerators and furniture off the back of that old flatbed truck with the help of the dolly. The dolly would not work on the washing machines. I would take the wringer off and lay the washer on its side on a moving pad and pull it to the back of the truck. Turning my back to the washing machine and reaching over my shoulders with my hands, I take the tub rim, and I would have the machine on my back and carry it to the house. Most of the time the miner's family would help me if they were home.

Of course, being seventeen, I wanted to show how strong I was. Some of the miners had a cow, a hog, or chickens. Bags of feed at a hundred pounds each were common items to be delivered. At that time, I liked to carry a bag under each arm to impress the girls. I don't know how I did it at 130 to 135 pounds. Today and 195 pounds, I would struggle with one of those hundred-pound bags.

I worked all through high school at the company store. I was in the distributive education program. I would leave school at about 1:30p.m. and drive my dad's car to the store. It was a seventeen-mile drive. My hours were from 2:00 to 6:00p.m., and thereafter if the work was not completed, I was paid for four hours of work, but most days worked longer than that. My starting pay was .55 cents an hour. It was not long until I was raised to .75 cents an hour. On Saturdays I worked until the store closed at 1:00 p.m.

Like all young men of that area and era, hunting and fishing were the only hobbies one had. I soon saved up enough money to buy my first shotgun, a model 37 Winchester 20-gauge. I still have that shotgun and killed my fist deer, a ten-point buck with it. My dad hung the mounted head in the company store at Leewood West Virginia. It remained there until I married and had my own home.

I missed out on a lot of activities in school as the job came first. This was a valuable lesson to learn at a young age. This premise enabled me to finish college and make a success out of everything I undertook in life. Not being involved in high school activities also probably kept me from getting married right out of high school as most of my friends did.

TURNING POINT
YOUR JOB COMES FIRST

You will never have to worry about finding a job with that belief. Coal miners were hard-working, good people. Most were people of their word, something sadly missing today. Some were rough and tough.

Fighting was as much a sport as anything else. If you stood your ground, they respected you. During the mine strikes, violence would erupt. Burglar alarms were installed in the stores. We lived in the store manager's house at Ronda, West Virginia. It was next to the company store. One night, when I was sixteen, the alarm went off.

Someone was in the store. My dad kept his cool and opened the shade without turning on the lights. He saw no car and knew the robbers were on foot. It didn't take long for three men to appear with large burlap bags over their shoulder. My dad waited until they were about sixty yards away. He was ready with his Winchester model 12 pump, loaded with No. 6 shot. He aimed just below the bags on their shoulder, and the rear pocket area of their work pants took a direct hit. They dropped the bags just as quickly and ran down the railroad tracks. We found a hat which we recognized as belonging to a union troublemaker. There was buckshot all over the bags of merchandise.

He had made a direct hit. The state police were called. Identifying the hat led to the arrest and conviction. The word spread that the store had a burglar alarm. My dad's job was to protect the store, and he did.

About two years prior to this incidence, my dad took me to Virginia with him, about sixty miles away. As we rounded a curve on the old winding road, there were men on a work detail. They were different from the regular road crews. They all wore the same clothing and had chains around their ankles. Standing above them on a rise were two men with shotguns. This was my first experience with prisoners. I was astonished and asked my dad what this was all about. He said, "Son, if you break the law this is where you will be." I never forgot that. I didn't want that, so I followed the law. That meant obey the speed limit, do not beg or steal, honor your commitments, and treat everyone with respect.

Turning Point
Make Following the Law a Daily Habit

I carried that principle into my adult work situations. I have had the unpleasant responsibility of terminating employees for dishonesty and lying. Up to this time, I had never been over sixty miles from home and the outside world.

I graduated at age seventeen from East Bank High School in 1952. The great NBA basketball star Jerry West graduated in 1956. I had a crush on Jerry's sister Hannah. Hannah got engaged before I could make any headway. She was married just out of high school. But I remember Jerry was a tall, skinny boy shooting baskets in the backyard. All my friends were getting married, leaving for the military, or leaving West Virginia for work.

I remember the other girl I had a crush on at Pineville High School. In the late forties, we did not have a telephone, so I went back to look for her. She also had graduated from Pineville High School in 1952. And after asking a lot of people about her, I tracked her to another company store. Much to my dismay, I was told she had got married and was gone. Two disappointments in a row. Later on, I will tell the story of how I ran into Betty by accident fifty-two years later. Both of us had lost our spouses. We had a long courtship, three weeks. We now have over eighteen years of happiness. More about this later.

Back to my work at the company store. What should I do? The Korean War was in full swing. My draft number was coming up in October 1953 when I turned in nineteen. Should I enlist? I didn't have enough money to go to college, my dream. I was now fulltime at the company store with the added responsibility of assisting my dad. He trained me to be the butcher and perishable manager. I was up to 90¢ an hour now, still paying room and board. Television was coming to Southern West Virginia. The first station was WSAZ channel 3 in Huntington. Mr. Gibson the store manager decided to put in a TV system for the coal camp. Roof top antennas would not work as the mountain, and the distance eliminated any signal. The mountain rose about two thousand feet above the coal camp. They were steep, full of trees, cliffs, coal dust, rattlesnakes, green briars, poison ivy, stinging nettles, and about anything else that would make you forget about television.

A right of way had to be cut up to the very top of the mountain. A tower was erected and lines with boosters were run back down to the coal camp at Acme West Virginia. There were no chain saws or modern equipment. We used brush hooks, picks, meat hooks, and hand saws. Sinking posts in almost solid rock was another challenge.

Mr. Gibson, his brother, Theodore, and I completed this project in 1952. After this project, I was ready to enlist in the air force and even took all the tests for flying. Mr. Gibson was a pilot and a pilot instructor during World War II. Just as I was ready to go, my dad was promoted to store manager at Leewood, West Virginia.

I was offered my dad's job as assistant manager and butcher, still not eighteen years of age. Wow, a pay raise was up to $1.55 per hour. This was a blessing in disguise as I could now save more money for my goal of going to college. The hours were long and hard, but I was eager to prove myself. I now had the job it took my dad twenty years to get.

Settling down to new responsibilities of making a profit and increasing sales were mine. Up to this point, I had just done what I was told to do. Now I had to make decisions only answered to Mr. Gibson. By this time, he knew I would get the job done, and he let me do it. My responsibilities included ordering everything in meats and perishables. Setting the meat case each day. The different cuts were put in pans in the meat case. Stores were 100 percent service at that time.

The customer would walk to the store with old-fashioned, lined shopping bags. They were primarily wives. A cut of meat, slices of lunch meat, cheese were weighed, wrapped, and tallied on a hand-cranked adding machine.

Most payment was in coal company script. There was very little cash. The script was like metal coins with the values from 1¢ up to $5.00. Five dollars would buy a lot of groceries in the early fifties.

Turning Point
Mental Work Does Not End
When the Day Is Done

Responsibility is twenty-four hours a day, not eight. You thought about what you had to do for tomorrow what you didn't get done today. You are tired both mentally and physically. This was an awesome experience for a seventeen-year-old.

I still found time for girlfriends. There was Patty, Carol, Chessie, Norma Dean, Wava, and two or three I cannot remember their names. Not bad for about two years of my life.

The TV cable was going strong. The cable fee was $2 a month for one station and still had snow at times. The store sold a lot of TV sets.

The early fifties models were heavy tube types usually in wood cabinets. The most prominent brands were Hallcrafter and Zenith.

Going to college was still in my mind as I could see in the future being a store manager was as far as I can go. After the Korean War ended in 1953, the mines started to slow down. Some were closed or consolidated.

At this time, I met two people who helped change my life and get me to the outside world. One was a life insurance salesman who sold me my first life insurance policy. I was fascinated how a whole life policy worked. The other was a professional executive with the Boy Scouts of America. He helped me form a Boy Scout troop at Acme., West Virginia. I was too young to be a scoutmaster at eighteen. Another man held the position, but I became the scoutmaster.

Turning Point
Being Involved in Something
Worthwhile Is Very Rewarding

Creed Wood was the executive's name. He encouraged me to go to college as a college degree was required for his job. This led me a year later to enter Salem College in Northern West Virginia. This was the other side of the world for me.

Scouting became a vital part of my life. My dad had been a cub master when I became a cub scout in 1942. I'm proud to say there have been four generations of scouts; my son achieved the rank of eagle. I became a professional like Creed Wood after college and Marine Corps days.

"Funny" things happen on the way to being an adult. In addition to the ones already mentioned, the following provide lasting memories. Now back to college.

In high school if you had a car, you were a celebrity. My friend Roy had a car. It was a 1946 Pontiac. We did like all sixteen to eighteen-year-olds did at the time—cruised on Saturday night. The roads were narrow and winding. We had been out and had struck out. Could not make contact with any girls. We were just driving those rural roads.

The night was pitch black, and there was no moon. We were approaching a railroad crossing that was rough. Roy slowed down to fifteen miles an hour; we were in no hurry. As we crossed the track, we suddenly hit something. For an instant, we thought a coal car was blocking the track. Stopping the car, we quickly exited to see what had happened. It was not a coal car but a mule fighting mad. He proceeded to kick Roy's car. Before he was through the grill, one headlight and several dents had been made. As quick as that, the mule just walked away, leaving us to survey the damage. Cars of that era were made of steel. Today, cars would have been much worse with plastic and fiberglass grills and fenders. It was not funny at the time, but looking back, how can you explain to a claims adjuster what happened? Lesson learned: beware of a mad mule. It was practical jokes in high school, not drugs and alcohol, that boys found intriguing.

During my senior year, I drove my dad's car to school as I had to work each day at the company store. One day my friends got inside the car, a 1947 Plymouth Special Deluxe, and put it in neutral and pushed it into the front entrance door of the school. Imagine being called out of class by the principal to explain leaving my car parked without setting the emergency brake.

Those same friends got me good at the senior prom. My date was probably the most popular single girl in the senior class. *She was the class president and very pretty.* After the dance, we were all going to Charleston to celebrate and eat at a real restaurant. I escorted Susanne in her pretty gown and corsage. I had brought her in my dad's car, a new 1951 Dodge Coronet. I was on top of the world. A new car, a pretty girl, the senior prom, and my first time to take a girl to Charleston. Usually a friend of mine would want to go with me as they didn't have the use of a car but not this time. I started the car and went about a hundred feet, and *bang*—a loud noise occurred under the hood of the car. Smoke filled the car, and Susanne and I made a quick exit. Much to my surprise, there were my friends all broken up with laughter. They had put a smoke bomb in the car. No damage, but it scared both of us. Susanne was not laughing. I never took her out again. Maybe they did me a favor. I had to go to college before I settled down. You can imagine a noise like a shotgun blast and smoke all through your car so thick you could not see. These same practical jokers, however, would be there if you needed them.

One time in industrial arts lab, a much larger boy who was a bully tried to take my place at the power saw. I was about 130 pounds and 5"10. He was about 6"2 and 200 pounds. Before I knew what happened, three of my buddies surrounded him and told him to get lost. He did. All for one and one for all is how it was done then.

Turning Point
Good Friends Are Vital in Life

Have at least six. If you die young, you will need them. Role models are very important to young men and women. Two other teachers stood out in my life. One was Mr. Morgan. He was teaching my sixth grade class. He led by example in appearance, speech, and actions.

He always wore a suit. He expected you to do your best and then some. I remember every day we sang at least one song. He had a good voice and used singing to get us out of our shyness and being bashful. He wanted each student to be their best.

The other teacher, Miss Gray, was a history and social studies teacher. She really got me interested in government and history. I had four classes with her in high school. I made As in all of them—about the only ones, I might say. She was an excellent mentor. Later on, I will comment on teaching and learning. Students will learn if they are interested in the subject. I firmly believe *self-motivation is the greatest force in life*. It should begin early in life and grow and grow and grow. The older one gets, the more important it is.

High school is over and reality sets in. Do I join the military? Do I stay with the coal company and work myself to be a store manager? Do I go into the mines? It's a lot more money.

Thankfully, none of the above, and I'm back to square one. I wanted to go to college but have only saved a few dollars. That was hard to do making less than $2.00 an hour as the assistant manager.

I was offered a job in the mines. If I did not like it, I could stay at the store. The pay was much higher. Why not?

My one day's experience was life-changing. The roof was not quite five feet in height. You worked bent over with your shovel. As I was bent over working, the roof cracked. A roof crack sounds like a pistol going off over your head. A drop of cold water hit the back of my neck. My mining career was over. There must be a better way to earn a living. God bless the coal miners, they will always have a soft spot in my heart.

The Island Creek Company Store and the "Stand" located at the forks of the road in Leewood.

Both my dad and mom managed this store at different times during their life. We lived beside the store.

Kayford Company Store

I worked there along with the Acme store. The Leewood and Acme stores were all within a five-mile area.

Pictures are courtesy of Bill Back, Mount Hope, West Virginia

CHAPTER 3

The College Years

With the help of Creed Wood, I applied at Salem College near Clarksburg, West Virginia. That was the other end of the world for me but by distance only about two hundred miles away. There were no Interstate highways, fast foods, or cellphones. It took about five hours to drive those winding mountain roads from our home then in Leewood, West Virginia.

I had my car paid for, a few clothes, and $537.00 dollars saved, enough for about one semester. There were no student loans, grants, etc. I knew I had to work as my parents could not help me. My father died at age forty-nine while I was at Salem. That almost ended my college days. The coal company gave my mother my dad's job. She was now the store manager. At least she could make it. My sister was fifteen and could not help.

Up to this point, I had never been very far from home and certainly in "Yankee County." There was big difference between northern and southern West Virginia. Families in the north had ancestries that primarily fought for the north in the Civil War. Mine had been part of the Confederacy.

I did not know where I would sleep that night. I was prepared to sleep in my car. Arriving in Salem was a little let down. It was a small one street town on US-50 west of Clarksburg. There were three or four colleges in the Charleston area. Most had modern buildings and looked like a college should.

I drove through town twice and did not see the college. Finally, I stopped at a gas station to ask for directions. "Where is Salem College?" The owner pointed across the street. There was an old two-story house that had a sign that said Salem College School of Music. I was shocked. What I gotten myself into? I had quit my job, two hundred miles from home, and had left for this place, *with my last girlfriend not very happy.*

I soon noticed two large brick buildings, and oh yes, across the street was a tennis court. There were about six buildings. Enrollment was about 450 at that time. Many of the students were local, and some commuted to school. There were no dormitories. Some old houses were converted into rooms, and there was only one large house where many of the girls stayed. I found this out quickly and after surveying some of the occupants, felt maybe it was not so bad after all.

You could tell the students that were freshmen. They had this funny green and white beanie cap. Where was the registration office? I asked the best-looking girl. She took me to the office, and I had made my first friend. The ice was broken.

My place to sleep that night was Jackson Hall just down the street. Jackson Hall was an old turn-of-the-century home with round rooms in the front and turrets. There were seventeen of us at Jackson Hall that fall of 1954. I was fortunate to share a two room and bath with three other boys. One was a junior, one a sophomore, and two of us freshman. Two of them were from the Charleston area, which made me feel right at all home. You could feel the excitement growing. This was going to be fun.

The year 1954 was a major change for the poor boy from Meeting House branch. As the Korean War was over, I still wanted to join the Marines. I decided to join the marine reserves and go for a commission when I graduated. I did this right after Christmas of 1954. Meanwhile I had to have a job to pay my bills. There were fewer jobs around the small town of Salem. My first job was washing dishes and cleaning up at a cafeteria. This was great as I got to meet a lot of students especially the girls. It didn't take long to realize there were pretty girls in Yankee County too. I was now working for 50¢ an hour. Do you suppose my dad was right? It was not long until I had my second job at the local Amoco gas station. Pumping gas, changing oil, and lubricating large trucks was dirty and not as much fun as working in the school cafeteria, but it would pay the bills. I made 50¢ an hour for a second time.

Being out of the isolation of the coal fields was wonderful. Meeting students from other states that came from different backgrounds was informative and uplifting. It didn't take long to realize *I was the only coal camp student on campus.* They had a *Who's Who* in the fifties that was happy and motivating to me. Fats Domino, Elvis Presley, Marty Robbins, the Penguins, the Platters, and the list goes on. Fine music was a sharp contrast to the Hank Williams, Hank Snow, and Red Foley and other country artists. I liked them both, the kind to the fifties fast and furious music. College life was great. I was making many new friends. Working two jobs and going to class kept me busy eighteen hours a day. Sleep occurred for the other six hours. *At one time I held three jobs.* More about that later.

Meanwhile back to my reason for coming to Salem. The American Humanics Foundation sponsored a unit at Salem to train young men and women to work with youth organizations as professional. Many of the students plan to work with the boy scouts, girl scouts, YMCA, boys' clubs upon graduation. This was the second year for Salem and to have this program. There were about twenty-five or thirty enrolled.

The founder of American Humanics Foundation was H. Roe Bartel of Kansas City, Missouri. Less than six weeks after I entered Salem, he was coming to visit. He came in October when West Virginia is beautiful beyond belief with all the fall colors. He took us all out on a weekend retreat to Lake Riley, which was a fun place to enjoy the scenery. We were assigned cabins and met in the meeting room for groups, conversation, etc. This was going to be great. I had never done anything like this.

All they had in the camps were the store and church. And besides there was Billie, Laura, Betty, and Dorothy who had caught my eye.

And those were just the Humanic students. This new life was great. My self-confidence was growing, and I saw a great life ahead of me.

Turning Point
I Came from Somewhere and I Am Going Somewhere I Can Do It

Now back to Roe Bartle. Everyone was stunned when he walked into the room. He was enormous, six feet and five inches tall, and weighed between 350 and 400 pounds. He did not need a microphone in a large auditorium. His booming voice was commanding. He was an orator second to none. Students were captivated by him. He was inspiring as he told Humanics stories. You hung on every word he said. He was a man's role model. He was a self-made millionaire, boy scout executive, mayor of Kansas City, Missouri, close friend and adviser to president Harry Truman, on the board of directors at several colleges and corporations.

The Blue Angles Navy pilots Mayors Office,
Kansas City, Mo. 1957
Pictured – Mayor H. Roe Bartel, Dick
Horwood, Micky Graham, Dallas Bailey

At this time, let me share what I learned about H. Roe "Big Chief" Bartel. He was instrumental in bringing professional football to Kansas City, hence the Kansas City chiefs, named after the "Big Chief." The stadium was called Bartel Stadium. Boy scouting was his love, and he believed in the Boy Scout program, making superior men out of average boys. He was keenly interested in governments and foreign affairs. Everything he became involved in, lives had a good purpose. He was a good man.

The major professor of Humanics at Salem was Weaver Marr a retired boy scout executive. Roe Bartel brought him to Salem, and Salem was a better place because of it. He also had the respect of the students. Professor Marr shared many stories about "Big Chief" Bartel. The others were told directly to me by Roe Bartel.

According to the "Big Chief," when Harry Truman made a decision to bomb Hiroshima and Nagasaki in World War II, here is how it was determined. President Truman had an emergency meeting of his cabinet, the "war cabinet." Top-secret information was presented including how devastating the atomic bomb was and what the horrendous casualties would be. The meeting lasted some time. Cabinet members asked questions and discussed every detail. President Truman asked each cabinet member to vote yes or no. Should we use this on Japan?

Each member struggled with the answer to the question. After some time to discuss, it was obvious they were divided and could not agree on a course of action. The secretary of war said, "Mr. President, we are divided as whether we should use this powerful bomb."

President Truman then stunned the cabinet with these remarks: 'That decision was made before we had this meeting. We're going to bomb *the hell out of them*." I did not like President Truman until I heard this story. He gained my respect. I can see why Roe Bartel knew Harry Truman. They were two of a kind— *powerful men who could make a decision*. I had become a republican by this time but had learned to respect two strong democrats, *Harry Truman and Roe Bartel*.

One other humorous story Roe Bartel told about Harry Truman was the president's love for roses. A foreign dignitary and his wife were visiting the White House. I don't know if it was a prime minister, a king, or who it was. But the story goes like this. President Truman and his wife Bess and daughter Margaret were escorting this couple on a tour of the White House and grounds. The president was proud of his roses. The foreign dignitaries' wife asked the president, "How do you raise flowers as beautiful as these?"

President Truman promptly said, "Roses have to have a lot of horse manure."

Later that evening Margaret asked her mother this question: "Can you talk to daddy and get him to use *fertilizer* instead of *horse manure*?"

Bess calmly said, "No, it took me forty years to get him to say horse manure."

Another story was how Roe Bartel got the resignation of a college president who became a communist in the late forties. The board of directors tried to get the president to resign, and he refused. He had a contract, and most boards were rubber stamps who lacked the courage to stand tall when needed. Someone got the idea to put Roe Bartel on the board. He soon realized the situation and told the board he would talk to the president and see if he would resign and avoid the public retaliation nightmare in the community of trying to fire him.

Roe Bartel and his attorney drew up the correct resignation letter for the president's signature. With that in his suit pocket, Roe Bartel made an appointment to meet privately with the president. Upon arriving at the president's office, he informed the receptionist not to disturb them. When he entered the office, he went over to a large brown credenza about six feet long and four feet high, picked it up, and blocked the only door out of the office. Roe Bartel emerged five minutes later with a signed resignation. I suppose it took four minutes to pull the president out from under his desk and rearrange the furniture.

My favorite story was when he was mayor of Kansas City. It seems as if prostitution and gambling were out of control when he took office. The "Big Chief" sized up the situation. He knew how to get things done. You didn't have to take a poll of public opinion and make decisions. He decided to go after organized prostitution. He summoned the chief of police to his office to discuss the problem. Politics as usual from the chief who gave you evasive answers.

Mayor Bartel then informed the police chief he had a plan to solve this problem. The police chief made the mistake of asking what the plan was.

Mayor Bartel said he was running an ad starting tomorrow in the Kansas City Star offering a $10,000 reward for any information on any ticketed prostitution that didn't result in an arrest and conviction. The police chief laughed and said how that would not help. Mayor Bartel said simply, "The first $10,000 reward I will pay there will be a new police chief the next day." Simple plan, quick result. That was Roe Bartel, a man of strong convictions and even stronger actions. He greatly influenced my life.

TURNING POINT
GREAT MEN HAVE THE COURAGE
OF THEIR CONVICTION

That has followed my life in making decisions always know what is right, and you will be a winner. The "Big Chief" returned every year to the retreats.

More about Salem college: At that time, it was a church school—Seventh Day Baptist. They worshipped on Saturday instead of Sunday. Chapel was required for thirty minutes three days a week. It was challenging and left you with a good feeling. Most of the professors were members of local churches. Smoking was not permitted on campus and alcohol was not tolerated. Class size was small. You got to know your professors and got individual attention.

It was a far cry from today's colleges where anything goes. We have lost a lot of our values today, and it is my opinion our education institutions' morals are compromised. Standards have been so very bent, if not broken.

A degree from Salem did not open doors to the business corporations or professions. *But it did prepare you for a life with purpose.* It wasn't *Harvard but it was heaven.* I graduated over sixty years ago. As I get older, I realize more and more how Salem enriched my life. The values the professors, students, and people in the town enabled me to live to my highest potential.

The freshman year was the hardest. Studying was hard to do. I had not done that in almost three years. The adjustment to an entirely different culture, new friends, and environments were in sharp contrast to the past. In the coal camps, life was day-to-day with very little change. There were not many positive hopes for the future. Salem college changed all that. I have found the driving force of life.

Turning Point
Enthusiasm
You Could Dare to Be Different with Your Beliefs and Enthusiasm

The sky is the limit. I've found out my grandfather's secret. Look for the good in people and lead by example. *Dream, dare, and do it.* Only one person will hold you back, and that is you. I had something to laugh about, dream about, and think about. I was on my way.

My life has been laced together with funny stories, mischief, and the first year of college was jam-packed with all those situations. Here are some that I still remember.

The false teeth fiasco. One of my friends had a set of false teeth. There were only two or three restaurants in town. One day four of us including Eddie, the false teeth owner, decided to get a sandwich.

This was a treat as we cooked for ourselves, and macaroni was getting old. We sat in the booth waiting for the waitress. She brought the menus and left. Eddie put the false teeth in the ashtray and placed a lit cigarette between the plates. The waitress returned, and we all had the menus over our faces pretending to read them. We ignored the teeth, and the waitress tried too. It was too much for her; she hurriedly went back to the kitchen. Soon three other heads behind the door were looking at the teeth.

As soon as no one was looking, Eddie extinguished the cigarette and put it back in his pocket to be used again. The waitress returned, the teeth were gone, and we acted like nothing had happened. Unless the waitress would laugh or ask questions, we ignored the whole incident. The word spreads in the community; it wasn't fun anymore. So Eddie worked the next angle, dropping an old plate in the commode of a restroom at the college when new students were present. He carried them in his shirt pocket. He got a lot of mileage out of that one as he would come out of the stall all excited, saying he dropped his teeth in the commode.

That was Eddie 1954. They were happy days, and that was West Virginia mountain humor. There will be many other examples later.

Pranks work part of college life. If you got a laugh out of it, we would do it. One of our four roommates was Ken, an upperclassman who was an organized neat freak. He had two pairs of shoes, lucky Ken.

He was out every night and woke us up when he came in late. He always slept to the last minute. He had a habit of switching shoes every day. The next day's shoes were placed beside his bunk ready to go. One of us, I won't say who got the idea, said, "Let's nail Ken's shoes to the wooden floor." We knew Ken had a 7:00 a.m. class the next day, so we slept in, waiting for Ken to put on his shoes. He couldn't figure out at first why his shoes would not come off the floor. We heard words from Ken that often were heard from the rough, tough coal miners. There is a difference when one is mad and not mad. Ken was the mad kind. With our blankets covering our hands and biting hard on the pillow, we slept through the whole thing. Ken got the message and was quiet when he came home late.

Another freshman project was the poll on Dear John letters. Almost all of the boys had left the girlfriend at home. I lost out in about ninety days; Eddie won the pool. He married the hometown girl after graduation. He was the only one who did not get a letter or broke up with the home girlfriend. Eddie became a Methodist minister, and I became a Baptist that year. After all, I did not want my minister to put his teeth in the commode. *Eddie was a great friend.*

The "panties" on the flag poll was perhaps the only place on campus that everyone saw. The housemother of the girls' dorm, as my dad would say, two and a half ax handles across the rear as she walked away from you. One of those rascal freshmen talked one of the girls in the dorm to secure one of the dorm-mothers' panties under the cover of darkness. These panties were hoisted up on the flagpole for everyone to see the next day. Everyone knew who they belonged to.

They never did catch the prankster. He later on was elected president of the class. This was fun we didn't have a flagpole at the coal camp but had plenty of panties that size. Oh I wish there had been a flagpole at the company store. Panty raids at colleges in the '50s was a big thing. One friend had an entire wall of his room decorated with panties and thumbtacks. Some were commented on.

There were some classes that were fairly easy. One can talk your way through. Others more than made up to difference. One was Biology I.

The professor expected 110 percent effort and got it. There were about seventy students in the beginning. The professor's opening remarks explained how he graded on the curve, how the grades were determined, and what he expected. At the end, he said, "Some of you do not belong in this class, and you will self-destruct." He was right. At the end of the second semester, about twenty had dropped out. I never worked so hard on any class. This was like working for the coal company. You did what was expected or else. I finished the class with a grade of C. There was one A and three B's. Being the top C did not make me feel any better.

Turning Point
Competition Brings Out the Best in You

I wasn't prepared for competition. I learned that working for the coal company. I was not going to be easy like high school. In order to get a degree, I would have to work my republican a—off, and I did both in the classroom and the jobs I held.

In a typical day was 6:00a.m. until midnight or later. During my senior year, I held three jobs, the last one at midnight, mopping and cleaning the restaurant. It took about two hours. The pay was two meals a day. I got my money's worth; the cook took care of me. I learned to get by with four to five hours of sleep. Even today six hours is a longtime. Why sleep your life away? Life is too interesting to miss, and there was always mischief and mayhem.

Another freshman class was an *Introduction to Philosophy*. The professor was Clifford Hansen. *He taught me the correct way to reason and think.* He had a brilliant mind. What I learned from his class paved the way for learning the rest of my college days and all my life. He too expected 110 percent. If I listed ten people who had the greatest influence on my life, he would be one of the fingers, if not the thumb. Many of the students avoided his classes, I'm glad I didn't.

Another C. If I can only get by this freshman year. Those two classes got me going, and I graduated on time, with a B plus average. I learned later in life that the B pluses of the world are the movers and shakers. Like Avis, they try harder.

The freshman year flew by. I had no steady girlfriend. I did not have the time or the money. I was beginning to establish my priorities in life. Too many dropped out of school to get married. I was not going to do that. The school year was ending, and I was broke but didn't care anymore.

Back to the coal company store. Jobs were hard to get in 1955 in West Virginia. If you were a registered republican, it was even harder. Mr. Gibson hired me back for the summer. I ran vacations and working three other stores. I also worked two to three weeks during Christmas breaks. The coal company Truax-Trayer was good to me, and I worked hard for them.

Things were not the same back home. Coal mines were closing, and coal company stores were closing. My high school friends were scattered, and many were leaving West Virginia for work or the military. I can hardly wait to get back to college.

My sophomore year in college proved to be my coming out period. I became interested in politics and a life of service. The vice president of the college was Cecil H. Underwood. He was thirty-three years old and had been elected six times to the state legislature. He decided to run for governor of West Virginia. We became friends, and he was a republican running in a state that had not elected a republican in my lifetime.

Cecil H. Underwood—Elected Governor of
West Virginia in 1956
Pictured— Micky Graham and Governor Underwood

Along with several of my college friends, we organized "*West Virginia College Students for Underwood.*" And we came up with the idea of selling our blood and donating the money to his campaign. *The Charleston Daily Mail*, one of the state's leading newspapers, picked up on the story. As chairman of my group, my name was in all the papers on why we supported Underwood. This was my first time to vote. You had to be twenty-one then, and I had just turned twenty-two. Despite all the odds, Underwood won, and we were jubilant. He was the youngest governor ever elected in West Virginia at age thirty-six. He ran again for years later for reelection, but the Kennedy era was on, and too many people voted a straight democratic ticket. He did run again in 1996 "at the age of 74" and was elected again and became the oldest governor in history. He held that feat that no one has matched—both the youngest and the oldest governor in West Virginia. He later helped me begin my insurance career. He was a good man and helped me develop my conservative values. He died in 2008 after a long successful life. He became a role model.

Students Sell Blood To Aid Underwood

Eight students at Salem College became professional blood donors this week to help a college official—Cecil H. Underwood—in his campaign for the Republican gubernatorial nomination.

Headed by a Cabin Creek resident, Mickey Graham, members of the Salem College Underwood-for-Governor Club went to a Clarksburg Hospital Wednesday in response to an appeal for blood.

They got $120, or $15 a pint, Graham said today, and "we've already opened a headquarters here in Salem."

"We didn't intend to take money for the blood, but the man insisted and we thought it would be a good idea to use it for the club," Graham said.

He added that the club members would distribute Underwood literature and help the candidate with his mailing campaign.

"We're 100 per cent for Mr. Underwood," the sophomore student of human relations told the Daily Mail, which newspaper, incidentally, he used to carry on Cabin Creek.

Graham is the son of Mr. and Mrs. A. L. Graham and his father is manager of the Truax-Traer store at Leewood. Underwood is vice-president of the college and now on leave of absence to seek the Republican nomination.

'HOUSEKEEPING' WEEK ENDS SAT.; DEPOSIT COUPONS

Good Housekeeping Week ends tomorrow.

The week-long sales event, sponsored by The Charleston Daily Mail, ends as the stores close at 5 p. m. Coupons for the 200 prizes being offered must be deposited by that time.

The prize drawings will be on the stage of the Virginian Theater at 9 p. m. Tuesday. Winners will be chosen for a vacation trip for two to Nassau, merchandise prizes of $200 and $100, sets of $50 bound Good Housekeeping books and 187 sets of reprints of features in the magazine.

Back at Salem, I became very involved in student life and student government. I was an officer in my fraternity, Alpha Phi Omega, and became the sports editor of the school newspaper, the *Green and White*. Grades were improving as I was learning to manage my time. Less time for girls and more for work and studying.

One of West Virginia's United States senators Jennings Randolph was on campus several times. He was a native and graduate of Salem. Salem's list of distinguished graduates is long. I got to meet and talk with Senator Randolph. This was beyond my wildest dreams.

I knew the governor and senator of my state personally. Senator Randolph was very likable and did a lot of good things for the college. He probably kept it financially afloat during some lean years. He was a US senator in Washington who sponsored the bill to lower the voting age to eighteen.

Branch Rickey was the next celebrity I met. He came to Salem to speak at a banquet. He was an impressive man. Mr. Rickey had been the CEO of the old Brooklyn Dodgers baseball team and was responsible for breaking the color barrier in baseball. He brought Jackie Robinson into baseball in 1947. It was only eight years later that I met him.

Mr. Rickey told the story how he prepared Jackie Robinson to play. A black man breaking into baseball was a problem. Many fans would taunt him. It was not going to be easy. Jackie Robinson came into Mr. Rickey's office and stood before his desk. He asked Jackie Robinson if he was ready to play and take the consequences. Jackie replied he was. At that point, Mr. Richey started calling him a vial names including the N word. He then said that is the way you will be treated and the only way you'll gain respect is how you play the game. Jackie did just that. He had passed Mr. Rickey's test and became one of the greatest players of all time. It's great men who make the world better.

I was beginning to rub elbows with people who had accomplished great things and were different from people I had known. Here is where I discovered the secret called the *belief and motivation*. Here is where I learned that truly successful people know what they want out of life. They have a plan to get there and are self-motivated. Add hard work and sound values and good ethics and nothing is impossible to achieve.

Being an officer in the Marine Corps was my goal. I enlisted in the US marine reserves. However, that was not the direction I was supposed to follow. More about that later.

Some of my freshman friends were dropping out. Money and marriage were often the reasons. Marriage was not a reason for me, but money could be. *I did everything to earn money.* One of my projects was the earthworm business. Armed with a flashlight and a bucket, I would go out at night to the places where these nightcrawlers would come out of the ground. Nightcrawlers are large earthworms which make excellent fish bait. I had a local bait store that paid me 1¢ for each worm. On a good night, I could make three to four dollars. Of course, the season for the worms was in the springtime, after the ground had thawed. I sold books and did odd jobs.

This sophomore year ended. It was time to look for a summer job. The coal companies were laying off people and closing stores. Luckily, an old friend that used to call on me at the store for wholesale produce had started his own business in Charleston. They sold wholesale fruits and vegetables all through the Kanawha Valley. I did everything that summer. My day started at 4:00 a.m. and ended between 3:00 and 4:00 p.m. It was about sixty hours a week mostly manual labor, unloading trucks and rail cars and processing orders for local delivery. Later on in the summer. I put on my only suit and called on stores and restaurants for sale orders. This was great experience, meeting people in selling.

The pay was good, and I made about $1,000 that summer for three months' work. This paid a lot of my college costs that year. It was time to go back to Salem for my junior year. I was always grateful for Mr. Frank Caputo for giving me that job.

Back in Salem, I was really into things. I worked with a local scout troop as an assistant scoutmaster. I taught Sunday school for the teenagers at my church. My Christian faith was growing. I was putting these thoughts into use and action.

Another fortunate event helped me to finish college. I received an athletic scholarship. I ended up managing the football and basketball teams. That paid for my tuition. I thought I was going to make it. Traveling with the teams and experiencing the athletic competition was an important chapter in my life. I was busy, I was in student government, elected vice president of the student council, and also did not have to worry about food. I secured a job mopping and cleaning a restaurant when it closed at midnight. They gave me two meals a day. I ate well those last two years—no more living on macaroni, cereal, and sandwiches.

The future looked bright. I was looking forward to graduation and a career as a marine officer. Then another major turning point came. I received a rare phone call from home. My mother told me my dad was diagnosed with cancer and would not live long. Bone cancer was deadly in 1957. I headed home to be the man of the family. My dad died shortly thereafter. My mother was two years younger than my dad at forty-seven, a widow with a fifteen-year-old daughter to raise by herself. Family came first. I would have to go to work and drop out of school.

Then a miracle happened—my mother was given my dad's job as store manager. The first woman I knew and may have been the only woman to ever manage and a coal company store. My mother encouraged me to go back to school. I only had fifteen more months to graduate.

It was back to school with a lot more dedication and direction. My grades improved. I worked hard and was now on a mission.

Experiencing death of a close family member at age twenty-two was sobering. No more pranks, life had a different direction.

TURNING POINT
LIFE HAS ROADBLOCKS—HOW YOU DEAL
WITH THEM MAKES THE DIFFERENCE

Many of my friends were graduating, getting married, and scattering. Most of them left West Virginia to pursue their careers or find work. The job market tightened up. It was time to find another job for summer.

A friend of mine who had recently graduated was hired as district scout executive in Ohio. With my scouting experience and background, he offered me a job as camp director for the summer boy scout camp. The camp was located on beautiful Leesville Lake in northeastern Ohio. It would be a ten-week job at $100 a week. That was a God-send. I could eat at the mess hall, and the tent was free.

I was twenty-two now and supervising a staff of volunteers ages sixteen to forty-five. Most of the staff were sixteen to nineteen-year-olds. These boys were just like I had been, full of mischief and mayhem. It was a new camp with only one building which housed the mess hall and provided the only permanent shelter. The rest of us were in tents. Most of the tents and equipment were World War II army surplus. We had one old jeep to go to town in. This experienced helped me for active duty with the Marine Corps.

Each week had a set of scouts arriving with their parents. The last night was parents' night. The camp did not have private toilets. When the mothers came and needed to visit a restroom, we had to improvise with a tent to put over the two-seater made on a wooden frame. A bag of lime was applied daily.

Boys will be boys. I discovered one particular night that something was going on at the women's toilet. An excited mother was running from the toilet to her car. That seemed strange to me as it would be more normal to run to the toilet. I went to the camp staff tent where we had the PA system. Two of my staff members were broken up with laughter. It did not take long to get an explanation of what was going on with the women's toilet.

Those two scouts had run a wire with a speaker into the toilet. The speaker had been carefully nailed under the seat out of sight. They would watch a woman go into the restroom. They would wait about thirty seconds or so and then in a loud gruff voice say, "*Lady, we are working down here.*" Needless to say, there was sitting room available very quickly. Apparently, the sign that said "Two holes, no waiting" took on an entirely different meaning.

Needless to say, I interrupted free speech and closed the radio station. It was all I could do to keep from laughing with them. This was the fifties, kids had fun, and laughter was the best medicine. The most interesting thing was that no women complained to me or told me what happened; they were too embarrassed. I had to admit that prank could have won an Oscar. I still laugh about it sixty years later.

Camp closed in early August, and I had about two weeks before classes resumed. I had to be back for football camp as I was now the manager and business manager for football and basketball.

One of my friends from Colorado had graduated in June and was getting married south of Denver in about ten days. He invited me and two other friends at Salem to the wedding. This was very exciting. I had a chance to go west. My mother let me take my dad's car for the trip. It was a 1955 Ford Fairlane four door sedan. I could not spend a lot of money. The three of us packed our sleeping bags and clothing, and away we went. There were no interstates then. We traveled old US-40 west. We slept in the car or on park benches on roadside pull-offs.

Going through a small town in Indiana, a truck forced us to change lanes to avoid an accident. My friend Dallas Bailey was driving. He had to cross the solid yellow line. Almost immediately a siren and flashing lights appeared, and we were pulled over. It was a local policeman who gave Dallas a ticket for improper lane change. We made our case that the truck forced us over, but the truck was local, and we were out of state and young kids. We were taken to a little building on the outskirts of town to a local *justice of the peace.*

Since I was president of my class, "the man" on campus, I acted as Dallas's defense attorney. The justice of the peace was a middle-aged man with a big belly and broad suspenders and belt, red flannel shirt and tobacco juice and stains in his beard. He hadn't shaved that day. He was like a lot of the elected officials that I have met in my life. He needed a job, and being a justice of the peace was better than working.

The justice of the peace was sympathetic to our story, but he said, "I have to find you guilty." The fine will be $1. I thought I had won the case. Then he said, "The court costs will be $15." He got a percentage of that. Since it was getting late in the day, I asked if we could work off the cost in jail. He quickly said, "The jail is full." They wanted the money. We thought it would be a great experience to tell our college friends we spent a night in jail. Sixteen dollars later, we were on the road again. That was a lot of money in 1957. A lot of bread and sliced baloney got us to Colorado. It took three days of hard driving, taking turns.

It was after ten o'clock that night that we saw the Colorado sign. We needed gas, but there were no towns, nothing for miles and miles. The gas gauge said empty. We passed a sign that said "Last Chance" Colorado. It was a little store and a gas pump. The sign said open at 6:00 a.m. We parked in front of the gas pumps and had our baloney sandwich and tried to sleep. It was a good thing we quit driving. It was over a hundred miles of Colorado badlands the next day before we found gas again. I know why they call it "Last Chance."

TURNING POINT
THE GOOD LORD LOOKS AFTER DUMB COLLEGE KIDS

Why, I don't know, but He does. Going to Colorado with very little money and less brains, someone had too. We got our friends married and ate to our hearts' content in our friends' home. His mother knew how hungry college boys were. I fell in love with Colorado. We took a side trip to Pikes Peak, the Garden of the

Gods. It was spellbinding. I made a vow for my future. I will be back to see the west. I have been doing that for over fifty years, visiting all fifty states and Canada.

Time to go back to Salem. I was now president of my senior class, the charter member of the Alpha Phi Omega, my service fraternity, earned my varsity letter, was the business and team manager of all three sports, football, and basketball and baseball. In addition, I was on the college debate team and served as an officer on four clubs and organization. I was busy, busy but managed to use my time wisely. It was at Salem that I developed a love for competition and being a winner. That "fire in the belly" would motivate me and all my endeavors in later life. It still does today that is why I am writing this book.

Nine senior students were nominated for Who's Who in American universities and colleges in1958. I was fortunate to be elected as this was done by the college. I was humbled and very thankful for this honor. The "*Tiger and Tigress*" award was given to a male and female student chosen by the senior class as the ideal students. Up to this point in my life, nothing can measure up to this award. I was elected "*Tiger*" by my fellow students. I was very grateful and humbled. Life was great. All the hard work was paying off. Soon it would end. But the best was still too come.

It was during these years that I met people who would have a great influence on my life. Each contributed in a different way and helped me to become different and directed in life.

First, Governor Cecil Underwood gave me an example of a poor farm boy who made it. Surely a poor boy from Meeting House Branch could do the same. Then there was Branch Rickey of the Brooklyn Dodgers and man who dared to be different. US Senator Jennings Randolph who graduated from Salem and was another poor boy from the mountains. I had the honor of introducing Governor Underwood and Senator Randolph at a banquet. It was a distinct and humbling honor Governor Underwood introduced me to the insurance business which I later spent over thirty years building a large agency.

Perhaps the life-changing event that motivated me more than anything else was meeting world-famous author, guru of positive thinking, *Napoleon Hill*. This was 1957, and he was eighty years old. I had never heard of him. Senator Randolph brought him to Salem. Senator Randolph gave Napoleon Hill credit for his motivation and success.

Dr. Hill was the principal speaker for the junior senior banquet, a big event of the year. Being president of my class, I had the honor of introducing him. His speech captivated me. I had never heard anyone more positive. This message was success and happiness. After the banquet was over, and we were exiting backstage, Dr. Hill came up to me with his outstretched hand. He looked at me and said, *"Young man, what are you going to do with the rest of your life?"*

I did not know how to answer that, no one had ever made me face that question.

He smiled and said, 'When you figure it out, this book will show you how to do it." This copy was a hardbound copy of *Think and Grow Rich*. He did indeed show me how to do it. Took me a few years to galvanize my thinking, goals, and direction. After reading his book, I realized why some people were successful and others were not. Outside of the Bible, I believe this book to be the greatest book ever written. He autographed the book with his distinct signature. I still have the book over sixty years later. It is one of my most valuable possessions.

This book was written in the Depression, challenging people to achieve and to live up to their dreams.

Dr. Hill spent a lifetime studying why some people become successful. The Carnegies, Rockefellers, Melons of that day were all inspired by Napoleon Hill. The book is still available at all bookstores and continues to sell after all these years. Sales are now over fifteen million.

All over the years, I have given copies of this book to young men and women who I thought might have that *"fire in the belly."* There have been several success stories. I will continue to do this as I meet young people.

I met a successful realtor in 2005 that knew all about Napoleon Hill. I told her I had an autographed copy of *Think and Grow Rich*. She immediately offered me $1,000 for it. The offer went to $1,500 dollars, but it wasn't for sale. I'll pass it down to my son, then pass it down, and hope it will inspire my descendants for years to come. The message is simple: successful people have strong beliefs and do what most people will not. *They dare to be different.*

Turning Point
You Become What You Think About

It was time to think "I can," not "I can't." Nothing is impossible, some things just take longer. The college years also taught me to *laugh at myself, my friends, and indeed the world.* Laughter is the best medicine to go with a positive attitude. This was tested at convention ceremonies. Governor Underwood was the featured speaker. It was an honor to be on the stage at the head table. The governor, president of the college, dean, professors, and their spouses faced the audience. Being president of my class, *I was given the honor of introducing the governor.*

As I was doing this, my friend and roommate was sitting in the front row trying to distract me. He had a pat of butter on his fork and was pretending to flip it at me. Unfortunately, he accidentally let it go. It did not hit me but hit the dean's wife in the forehand, and it stuck. Talk about being lost for words. The dean's wife saved the day. She calmly took her napkin and removed the butter. If you can introduce the governor of the state with this handicap, you can do anything. It was time to kill a roommate.

It was during this time I met another person whom changed my life. I had joined the first and only Baptist church of Salem as a freshman in 1954. In the fall of 1957 after returning from Colorado and football camp, I settled into my senior year of college. There was a new Sunday school class at church, the college and young people's class.

It was early in October 1957. For the first meeting, we sat along tables facing each other. The teacher was to my left at the end. I was across from a beautiful shy girl that I did not know. We introduced ourselves. Everyone was connected to the college in some way except this pretty young woman. Each couple there were either engaged or going steady. That pretty girl across from me had just returned from her freshman year at Bowling Green, Kentucky, now Western Kentucky University. Each one of the couples indicated this was my soulmate, boyfriend or husband. When it was my turn to speak, I gave my name and said, "I'm still looking for a girlfriend." I looked directly at this young woman, and she dropped her eyes and blushed. She had my attention. It was too late, and a turning point in my life had begun.

Her name was Margaret Nutter, better known as "Margy." She was a native of Salem with a long family history in Salem. Up to this time in my life, I had dated or gone steady with sixty-seven girls, believe it or not. Most of the time the girls found a new boy-friend after meeting me. I guess I scared them with my ambitions and strong beliefs. I thought I could do anything I set my mind to and still do. Now I'm going to be a writer.

It didn't take the two Sundays to ask Margy to go to the movies with me. She blushed and said okay. That was November 10, 1957. We had a second date two weeks later. I still had to scrape enough money for two movie theater tickets.

That night I made a quick decision: this was the woman I would marry. Once I made up my mind, I was on a mission. For some unknown reason, she said yes, and we were engaged thanks-giving 1957. I had a lot to be thankful for, but we could not get married because I had six more months of college, no money, and the Marines staring at me in the face.

I graduated from Salem on June 3, 1958 at 10:00a.m. in the morning as the senior class president and had a lot of responsi-bility for the ceremonies. Margy and I got married the same day at 6:00p.m. that evening. *What a day!* I had been working for the A&P in Clarksburg in the evenings and Saturdays, making about $50.00 a week. Margy went to work for the Harris County

Prosecuting Attorney in Clarksburg. She made $50.00 a week salary.

We had more faith than brains. When is the right time to get married? There never is a right time to, it's just the right thing to do, and if you believe, it will work. It did for forty-three years. Sadly in June 2001 I lost her to diabetes. We had gone through many trials—cancer, amputations, diabetes, and you name it. Until death do you part. We believed it and lived it. She was my motivating force for those forty-three years.

Wedding day Micky
and Margy 1958

Margy the
beautiful

With all the grandchildren

My sister Mary Sue, My
mother Ethel, and yours truly

VOTE FOR

A. L. "AL" GRAHAM

REPUBLICAN

House of Delegates

MAY 11, 1948

THANKS

Either I inherited it or it just rubbed off on me,
but my Dad also had that *"fire in the belly"*

My High School
graduation
picture "1952"

CHAPTER 4

After College—Life Has Just Begun

We had been married a month waiting for my letter to go to Quantico, Virginia to get my commission as a second lieutenant in the Marine Corps. My commanding officer had sent a letter recommending my appointment. I graduated with better than a 3.0 average, had been a student leader, and passed all the physical and mental tests. I even qualified for pilot training. I was still working for A&P as a produce clerk.

Then like a bolt out of the blue, the letter came. I was not selected. There had been a great reduction in the slots, peacetime, and I was not needed. I can stay in the reserve, wait, and try again. This probably was one of the biggest disappointments of my life at the time. I still regret it; I wanted to be a marine officer.

TURNING POINT
LIFE IS NOT A BED OF ROSES

A college degree is not a guarantee for success. What do I do now? Seems like in college I knew all the answers. Reality had set in. I was married with responsibility to provide for my wife. I had hit a roadblock. It has been said in college, there is no humility.

After graduation, and you're out of the fishbowl, into the ocean, humility hits you hard right in the mouth.

I had always found a job and will to do so again. However, more humble and concerned. During this period from June through September 1958, I had to go to summer camp at Little Creek Naval Base Virginia for amphibious training. It was there that an event changed my life.

The 77th Rifle Company, Marine Corps Reserve, of Zanesville was judged the best performing military unit in the Armed Forces Day Parade Saturday.

Micky in uniform
Feb. 1962

Eisenhower was president, and there was trouble in Lebanon. We were taking training on helicopter landings when the pilot landed and informed all of us to get back to the barracks at once. Something was up! The sirens had started and we fell into formation and the company commander told us the base was locked down. The president had ordered Marines to Lebanon. I was in the infantry company. I thought this was it. We were all issued ammunition and told to lock and load.

No one knew what was happening. Our company did not deploy but most of those there were. I watched the ships leaving port. A sick feeling in my stomach. The gates were all secured. No one could leave or enter the base without clearance. Even civilian employees could not go home. We were told to pair off. With my loaded M1 rifle, I was assigned to a jeep and driver. We were in a group to patrol the beach area. We were to stop anyone found there and detain. Order was given to *shoot to kill anyone that resisted*. For the first time in my life, I was not in control.

It was about 4:00 p.m. civilian time. We had been taking hard training all day. We had sweated through our clothes, hungry and scared. All night long, we were up and down the beach area. Only two people were apprehended. A naval ensign and his girlfriend, both drunk and out of uniform. They sobered up in the brig until they were cleared. Quite a night. No sleep, scared, dirty, and hungry. It was there I realized the great sacrifice our military men and women make. Everyone should have the experience I had. We were sent back home after our training better Marines and men.

The search for a job of any kind was on. I began to think my dad was right. I would be making less money than I was before I went to college, only now they were two mouths to feed and a widowed mother and baby sister to be concerned about.

In late August, I finally got a job offer that required a college degree. I had a degree in human relations with minors in English and sociology. Today that would be a degree in social work. The job was with the West Virginia health department. A letter came from the state director offering me this position. The title was "Venereal disease inspector II." I guess I wasn't qualified to be "venereal disease inspector I."

The salary was $300 a month and 8¢ a mile for car reimbursement. There were no Interstate roads, and it would require extensive traveling over the mountain roads. My old car would not last long. I would have netted less money than the A&P job when you ordered meals, motels, etc. I respectfully turned it down. I still have the letter framed in my office. My son and three grandchildren have a copy, and I have told them the story too many times. *Guess what*, when they graduated, they found out maybe grandpa knew what he was talking about. In today's world, a college degree will not get you on easy street at once. *Lesson learned.*

State of West Virginia
DEPARTMENT OF HEALTH
CHARLESTON 9

November 26, 1958

Mr. Alfred L. Graham, Jr.
501 Preston Street
Clarksburg, West Virginia

Dear Mr. Graham:

Your name has been referred to this Bureau by the State Merit System as being available for the position of Public Health Venereal Disease Visitor II.

The salary for this position is $300.00 per month. Considerable traveling is involved and a rate of .08 cents per mile is paid by the State for personal cars used in business activities.

Persons employed in this capacity must be free to accept assignment in any county or group of counties in the State. The job consists of activities involving interviewing persons diagnosed as being infected with a venereal disease for contacts, finding named contacts and persuading them to have an examination for diagnostic purposes and treatment if found infected, participating in blood testing programs, and health education activities.

If you are interested in accepting such a position, will you please come to my office on Monday, December 1, 1958 at 1:00 p.m. for an interview. We are located on the fourth floor of the New Office Building, Room 447, 1800 East Washington Street in Charleston.

Very truly yours,

Paul D. Kates
Paul D. Kates
Health Program Representative
Bureau of Venereal Disease Control

PDK:is

Being a registered republican in the fifties in West Virginia was like Elizabeth Taylor going to the convent to be a nun. Not likely to happen. Even a job with the county, city, or state was not considered if you were a republican. In small towns, a registered republican could not get a job unless you work for a company or another republican or business. The unions ran West Virginia especially South West Virginia.

My friend and vice president of Salem College, Cecil H. Underwood, was now governor of West Virginia. He was the first republican governor since before the great depression.

He was elected in 1956 as a result of the Eisenhower landslide. I had headed the "*Students for Underwood*" for his campaign. We had *sold our blood* to raise money for him.

He never forgot his friends at Salem College. I contacted him for help in finding a job which led me to a major turning point in my life. He got me an interview with New York Life Insurance company. I was hired at once and found a career that later made my life complete. More on this later.

The marine stories that I'll never forget: the first chow at Paris Island. With my food tray in line, I paused to smile at the one serving SOS *beef gravy on toast*. Big mistake, most of the SOS landed on my bare wrist and forearm. Moral: do not smile and keep a line moving.

First ever flight on an airplane: my company was being flown to Camp Lejune for advanced infantry training. The plane was an old flying boxcar from World War II and used to transport troops and supplies. A fold-up canvas bench was on each side. The restroom was a rubber tube on each side in the rear. It had a small cup at the top with the tube going to the outside of the plane. You had to have a steady hand and pray the plane didn't hit an air pocket as you are using it. To this day, when I am outside in a clear sky and moisture hits my face, I look up to see if a plane was flying over.

We had our field packs, rifle, and parachutes although I had never had any training on how to use a parachute. It was a beautiful sunny day, and we were flying into a brilliant sun. The flying boxcar had portholes on each side.

Bouncing around in a plane was a new experience for me. I had gone from one day in the coal mine to being over the earth and not under it.

The captain of our company, a battlefield commissioned officer of World War II, was letting one man at a time go to the cockpit to observe. Probably 90 percent had never been on a plane.

My turn came. Upon opening a door, this was the scene. The plane was on automatic pilot, a poker game was in progress with the three crew members. A fifth of Old Granddad was open, and all three were drinking. The crew was leftover World War II survivors and had the facial scars to prove it. They had been to hell and back in the Pacific theater. Strike two. Strike one had been the air pocket we hit. Hoping I did not need a relief move from the tubes in the rear, I headed back to my canvas seat, pack, rifle, and parachute.

Within a couple of minutes, the plane lurched and shook. *Almost strike three.* The tubes won't work. We kept losing altitude. I looked through the porthole. The starboard motor was on fire with black smoke billowing out. The order was to get your chutes on. I was way ahead of everyone. All I knew from seeing war movies was to count to ten and pull the cord when you jump.

The poker game ended, the whisky stored, and the pilot took control. It was an oil fire. He feathered the engine, and we came in on one motor. I have always been partial to seasoned marine fighter pilots who drank and gambled and God knows what else. They get the job done.

I was serving under a sergeant who had the C.M.H. Congressional Medal of Honor from World War II. His name was Herschel W. Williams, a five-foot-six man and about 150 pounds. I did not know he had the congressional medal. We were at the Little Creek Naval Base at Little Creek, Virginia, taking amphibious training. One day we were ordered to stop training and report to the parade ground. It was a hot July day in 1958. No one knew what was going on, but we were glad to take a break from the tough training.

We were at parade rest in our fatigue uniforms. The order was "Ten-S-Hon." Out walked a general, and I thought it was going to be a *strike four*. What was going on? Our commanding officer in a loud voice said, "Sergeant Williams front and center."

Sergeant Williams came forward, and we all saw for the first time the medal of honor around his neck. Wow! We knew something special was about to happen.

With everyone at attention, stunned, and spellbound, the general read how Herschel W. "Woody" Williams from Quite Dell, West Virginia qualified for the medal of honor.

It was on the beaches of Iwo Jima. The Japanese were in underground caves and pillboxes in Mt. Suribachi. As our Marines landed, they opened up with a rain of fire. The beach was lined with dead and wounded Marines. The Japanese had to be smoked out of those caves. Flamethrowers were used to accomplish this. They were strapped on your back like a backpack and made a dangerous target for the enemy. Little progress was being made, and a bitter price was being paid. Many Marines were killed as the enemy would shoot the tank. It would explode, and the marine was part of history.

Woody was a twenty-three-year-old marine reservist. He saw many of his buddies killed. He strapped on a flamethrower, and up the hill he went. Two riflemen followed him to provide cover. Both riflemen were killed. As he grabbed a flamethrower, another marine heard him say, "We all have to die sometime," and off he went, returning several times for a new tank. When it was over nearly five hours later, the offense to take Iwo Jima was starting to make headway.

Everyone was stunned to witness this. Then the general read the following statement: "Sergeant Williams, by the order of the president of the United States Dwight D. Eisenhower, you are now a commissioned warrant officer."

What a privilege for me to have been there and serve with this great man. I have a copy of the C. M.H. citation, his autograph, and the lifelong friendship. He is still alive today and past ninety years old. He is the only living survivor of twenty-seven Marines to receive the medal of honor at Iwo Jima.

He later became a chaplain and veterans administrative executive. America's great generation. I was proud to be a marine.

When "waterboarding" headlines were heading the country as we sought for intelligence to fight the Taliban, I was reminded of a "waterboarding" incident in the Marine Corps.

Escape and evasion training—all those critics and *liberal media* might just learn something if they had ever served in the military. I was at Camp Lejune, North Carolina, taking advanced infantry training. In escape and evasion training in the field, you are to infiltrate a large wooded area. The objective was to get through to a prearranged destination. The enemy, the Marines, were waiting in the woods, hidden, waiting for you. Needless to say, we were all captured. We thought it was a joke at first. We were taken to a simulated prisoner of war camp. The enemies were six big Dis with "swagger sticks." "Get out of those clothes now," they barked out like grizzly bears.

What, I am not going to take off all my clothes in this ninety-five-degree sun in front of God and all these witnesses. I hesitated a few seconds and this Di came over and said, "*Now*" and with that, he hit me a cross the shoulder with his swagger stick. Down I went. I have always made quick decisions. In the coal camps, I never backed down from a fight, but now taking on six mean Dis was not for me.

Off went my boots and clothes. Standing in the hot sun naked was humiliating enough, then the remarks and smirks that followed. Or worse, it is that a man's ego shrinks along with other things. We were marched off to a stockade made of wooden slats about three inches apart. It was so narrow you had to enter sideways. You were belly to buttocks against wooden slats.

Look out for splinters. Hot sand burned our feet. The top was over about three feet above our heads. Without any warning, the floodgates opened above us, and we were deluged with thousands gallons of water. Oh, to be back in that bathtub that hung on a nail on the back porch. You can't move some nearly panicked. You thought you would drown. Each Di came in front of you, asking questions about everything. We gave name, rank, and serial number only.

One Marine was telling them everything just get me out of here. They did, and in front of us he was spread-eagled on sheets of hot tin face up. He was ready to confess even killing the president. *They had made a point.* The water stopped, and we were released. We thought, *Not so fast.* Suddenly buckets and buckets of hot sand were poured out on our wet, naked bodies. You had to close your eyes to keep the sand out. I made it with most of my company without giving anything but name, rank, and serial number. A strong bond was growing between us. Outside of sand everywhere and a sore shoulder, I had survived.

It was not torture. My hat's off to the military and Vice President Cheney for their actions with the Taliban prisoners. I would like to have the chance at my advanced age to waterboard them.

I only know of a small handful of the Marines in my company that are still alive. Only two of us did not smoke or drink. We are both still going, but each lost our wives.

There are many stories a serviceman or woman can tell. In summary, I am not only proud to be a Marine I credit my experiences and training as valuable as college, parents, and friends helping me to achieve anything worthwhile in life.

I was discharged in January 1963. My son was born in the same year. My old company went to Vietnam. Some didn't come back. One of my best friends in high school was Kenneth Shadrick, the first man killed in Korea.

My family has a history back to the revolutionary war. My great-grandfathers fought in the confederacy. My great uncle was in World War I. My Uncle Charlie was an eighth-grade dropout who joined the army in 1937 and made colonel. I mentioned him earlier. My first cousin O.J. Gill was in World War II, Korean War, and Vietnam. He was discharged as a Lt. Colonel.

I am proud of all of them. The Grahams came from Scotland (what the king didn't hang) to America, and the rest is history. You probably know why I wanted to be a marine officer. I had to settle as we used to call them buck sergeants.

CHAPTER 5

The Move Out of West Virginia

At last, I was a licensed life insurance agent. It was better than trimming produce or venereal disease inspector II.

This turned out to be my true calling in life. Doing things for people that they needed and could not do themselves. I was young and still had a lot of maturing to do. The more gray hair you have, the better it prepares you to market life insurance. It would take another nine years to settle back in the business. Several factors prompted my decision to leave Clarksburg, Salem, West Virginia area.

One that really bothered me was I came to Salem College to prepare myself to be a professional with the boy scouts of America. That seems to be an officer in the marine corps. When I hit a roadblock there, I had to have a job. I did well in my seven months with New York Life, made more money in seven months and I had ever made in a year. I felt guilty; I wasn't using my degree. Little did I know at the time that adequate insurance for families was a need that most family's neglected to fulfill.

Another factor was that we were too close to in-laws. Although we had a cordial relationship, I resented the remarks that nothing good ever came out of the "southern part" of the state. "You are not feeding my daughter," "You'll never amount to much." Plus many suggestions we did not need. Being a republican marrying into a strong democratic union family was a challenge. I felt like "meathead of all and the family show" except I was a conservative and "Archie" my father-in-law was a strong democrat. Margaret's grandfather Charles Nutter liked me. He would tell people, "Margaret got herself a good man, he is a republican." He was a republican living with his democrat son—not a healthy situation. He also was instrumental in helping me to become a Mason. I am proud to say I am a thirty-second degree mason for over fifty years.

The decision was made to try the Boy Scouts of America. Several of my college friends were now fulltime with the boy scouts. One of them told me about an opening in Zanesville, Ohio. That was about a hundred-forty miles away on winding down roads in 1959.

I went to Zanesville to interview and got the job. I had to go to school for forty-five days at Schiff Scout Reservation where they trained the professionals in New Jersey. Hard on a marriage. Leaving Salem area was hard on Margaret; her family had been there for several generations.

Jobs were scarce in the late fifties and early sixties. I took a possible pay cut although I was on commission with New York Life.

My starting salary was $4,100.00 per year. That was about $41.50 per month more than *venereal disease inspector II*. At least I would not have to wear rubber gloves. Scouting is a wonderful program for boys. I soon learned my job was working with the institutions, men, and businesses. Money and manpower in organizing volunteers was my primary responsibility. Margaret managed to get a job as a criminal secretary with the county prosecutor's office, one she held for twenty-seven years until retirement in 1993. She loved it. I was working days and nights. We could not start a family or buy a house for a long time.

After a year, I realized business was more interesting and challenging. I was offered a new job selling building materials at $1,000 more each year. I was on a salary and loved it. I traveled about three counties. In the early 1960s, the economy went into the tank and the company I was with almost went under. We sold overhead doors and windows, building came to a halt. The salary went to commission only.

Oh, oh, another roadblock. Three jobs in three years. Had my dad been right, or was my father-in-law right? I cannot hold a job. I must be driving my wife crazy.

She is settled, likes her job, and the economy has no effect. She has a government job. Strange couple—a conservative republican married to a democrat family. I used to say I have been a republican all my life that married a democrat. But I would add, I turned her over the first night. Looking back, she was as conservative as I was, just kept her mouth shut. Me with my big mouth was enough for one family.

CHAPTER 6

My Teaching Time

We did not want to leave Zanesville as we were active in our church and had made many friends. I took a part time weekend job at the newspaper, *The Times Recorder*, working weekends to cover obituaries and news. *It was there I formed a love for writing.* After all, I had a minor in English and wrote with West Virginia humor.

Finances were tight a degree in human relations did not open doors to higher-paying jobs. Someone told me I could get a job as a teacher in Adamsville about twelve miles away. I contacted the county school superintendent A.O. Tom, a fine gentleman I greatly admired. He offered me the job. I just had a temporary certificate and must enroll at Ohio University for more classes to be certified, which I did.

Adamsville was a small rural high school whose students were from farms or factory workers. They were great people and I loved the kids. My salary would start at $3840 a year. I got two years' credit for military time. That was my lowest-paying job I had out of a college. I was thankful to have a job.

I was the third English-History teacher in that year. The month was January and I soon found out why. Those high school boys were rough and tough. The prior teacher could not control

84

the classes. English 10, 11, 12, US History, and World History were my classes.

The year 1960 was quite a year to be alive. The space program was starting, and John Glenn was from New Concord Ohio just fifteen miles away. I used that in my classes to get the kids interested. Most of the classes were farm kids raised with good manners and respect for authority. Two or three were not raised with respect for anything.

When I walked into the first classroom of English, they were waiting for me. I had been in the office for orientation. I was going to be tested.

The ringleader of the athletes, who did not open a book and ran roughshod over everyone, said, "*What is your name, Shorty?*" He was a big boy.

"Come with me," I said, out the door, and down to the principal's office. Paddling was still allowed in 1960. One hung in the principal's office with holes in it. I know how to use it as it had been used on me when I was in high school. Now was the time to take control of my class.

I said, "Bend over and grab your ankle." He wore tight blue jeans. I let him stay in that position about a minute. "Turn about half a turn to the left." Another wait. "And turn another half turn." This went on for about three or four minutes with his rear-end sticking up in the air and his head looking at the floor.

He blurted out, "What in the world are you doing?"

I replied, "I want to do this just right, I want to enjoy it." Got a snicker from the secretary to the principal. He received the board of education three times. There is an art to paddling. Just as you are about to make contact with blue jeans, you tip the paddle slightly to the right. The results are like a sting. It can bring tears without damage. Our trip back to the classroom was very quiet.

Bob was very teary-eyed, and all the girls were holding their hands over their mouth to hold back the laughter. My name was Mr. *Graham*, not Shorty. No more disciplining problems, only motivation problems. Bob later became a successful businessman.

I met him several years later. He shook my hand and called me Mr. Graham. I told him I was proud of him.

Our schools began to change in the '60s—in many ways not for the good. Of course, our entire country was changing.

Athletics and not academics was first on the priority list. Small school districts were consolidating. *Small towns decayed when their schools closed for social prominence was coming in and basics were going out.*

The great society began, and we're paying for it today. The old adage I grew up with, if you don't get an education, you'll have to dig ditches for a living was replaced with *you can do your own thing or anything and get paid for doing nothing.*

Looking backward, I see where it started. Parents said, "I don't want my kids to have to work like I did. They don't have to do anything if they don't want to!" My father said, "At seventeen, you're a man, act like one." That will be $60 a month room and board in 1951. He did me a favor. I didn't know that until I had a son.

I loved teaching. If I were rich, I would have worked for free. Teachers in the school fell into classes. 1. Those that did the minimum and could not compete in the real world. Usually those classes were anything they want. 2. Teachers who wanted their students to learn and were in charge of their classroom.

No wonder many of the students chose the first type class teacher. It was the easy way out, and they were not mature enough or had parents who insisted on performance. Hopefully I qualified for the second group. Several times I heard students talking to classes coming up: "Don't take Mr. Graham's class, he is too hard or too mean." I liked both descriptions.

The boys who played basketball in that small school were the heroes. They soon learned their teachers would pass them with a C average, even if they slept through the class.

Then came along that mean Mr. Graham. In all my classes, I had developed a detailed plan of how the grades were determined—written work, oral participation, certain percentages, assignments on time another percentage, extra work, a percentage, tests every Friday, a percentage. Each Monday, they should know exactly what their grade was.

This was revolutionary. The A students in the past were falling into the B area. Those athletes with one exception fell to F as they did nothing.

Each Friday was test day. I was stumped how to motivate the boys who did nothing. I did not have a problem with the girls. I came up with the idea of the "stooges row." So every Friday, Moe, Larry, and Curly would come up to my desk. Bring their books, notes, whatever, and cheat. The girls were laughing at them, and that was good. I did not put any boys in the stooge's row that were not bright or had a handicap. I would say to them, "The three of you together can't make seventy," and they couldn't. *Wow.* This opened Pandora's box. They didn't want to be on stooges row next week, let alone have the girls laugh at them. They started to study. That would not work today. I would be violating the rights, contributing to a nervous breakdown and everything's the ACLU or some lawyer could dream up. There were two or three boys who really grew quickly, I was proud of them.

I had their respect. I was still in the local Marine Reserve Corps. I was a very lean and mean Marine. I'm still mean but can't see my circumcision scar anymore.

The girls were another story. They were more mature less aggressive and more receptive. I have a theory that boys be seven years old to start school and girls should be six. Might be worth a try.

One girl in particular, Robin, came from a family of modest means with very little motivation. They were poor but humble. Robin was the best student I ever had. She aced everything and went the extra mile. One paper she did, I gave her an A minus.

You would have thought the end of the world had come. She stayed after class and asked why I had given her an A minus. What could she do to get an A? I loved her. She went on to college and earned her doctorate. She was exceptional. Other girls use their looks and charms to get grades. That didn't work with me.

I was twenty-six when I started teaching. Some of the girls were eighteen in the senior class. One in particular made it very obvious that she had other things on her mind. This girl or woman found out after a brief lunch, I would go back to my room and grade papers or prepare for a class. She started coming in to talk. The talk was not about school.

She made me very nervous. One day she came in, pulled her dress to her waist, and said, "Do you think I have pretty legs?" That did it. Do not be alone in your room. She then started calling my home at night.

Margaret said, 'Who is this girl that is always calling you?" She called sometimes when I wasn't there. I explained the situation the best I could. The next time she called, she had a wife to talk to. No more calls after that.

Now in our school, we read stories of teachers being sexually involved with students. It happened with male teachers in my time. Now it's good-looking, young female teachers. Thank God, I was too busy pursuing girls and was afraid of their daddies. That is called a check and balance system. It worked. Almost all my teachers in high school were graduates MMU—middle-aged, mean, and ugly. I was lucky.

One of the biggest disappointments in my two-year career as a teacher and led me to leave teaching was intervention by the principal to change grades on the basketball players. He was a politician afraid to take a stand. He said, "Don't you think you have made a mistake on those grades?"

I answered and said, "No, but you will." At that point I made up my mind: *you have to be true to yourself.*

I remember what my dad said in 1948 when he ran for the state legislature as a republican. His boss came to him and said, "You won't have a job if you do this."

My dad's comment was "I won't have a job." He ran anyway but lost in a close election. Republicans and Wyoming County were outnumbered about five to one.

He told his boss, "I will pick sh—with the chickens before I will compromise my principles." I believe it rubbed off on me, and my life opened up. I loved the kids. Later on in life I was president of the PTA in another district, elected to two four-year terms on the school board. I served as president when my son graduated and had the great privilege of presenting him with his diploma.

CHAPTER 7

The Kroger Story

It was now 1962, out of college four years, five jobs counting A&P part-time or six counting my stint writing for the newspaper.

The year 1962 began with *a big turning point* in our lives. We had tried to start a family for three years. At last Margaret became pregnant. Our son Alan was born January 3, 1962. Just missed the 1961 income tax deduction. It was a difficult birth. Dr. Bobby Young had to place a tube in his throat and breathe for him for over twenty minutes. He did not give up, and Alan started breathing on his own. I was in the waiting room at 3:00a.m. where I had been all night. You could not be present for the delivery in those days.

The waiting room was empty. There was no one to give you a report. About 3:15a.m., Dr. Young came out with a *grim* look on his face. I was scared far more than being on the plane with the engine on fire. Dr. Young explained what had happened. I would not be able to see the baby until late that evening as he had a ruptured blood vessel in his head and was in intensive care. He was on a "rocker" when I finally did see him. His color was blue-black. It did not look good.

Margaret pressed the doctor and me as to what was wrong. She had never held her baby. I brought Margaret home three days later, but Alan remained for a week. We could only see him through the glass window. Everything else was normal except he had six toes on one foot. He would have to have one removed later. Unfortunately, the wrong toe was removed. He has adjusted well as an adult. However, he would never be able to join the Marines. More about that later.

TURNING POINT
BE THANKFUL FOR CHILDREN

We never could have any more children. My salary as a teacher was now $3960 per year. Margaret was forced to go back to work to make ends meet. I still have the newspaper job. It was time to make the tough decision. By this time, I was *administrative "first" sergeant* of my reserve unit in Zanesville. The commanding officer Captain Robert Shafer told me he was taking a job with the Kroger Company as a manager trainee. It sounded good to me. An interview was scheduled in the Columbus Ohio office. I was hired at a fabulous salary of $5700 per year. My years working in the coal company store and A&P had prepared me. I learned every department and the store including the night stock crew— you did it all back then.

In six months, I was promoted to co-manager at store N-153 in Zanesville. I had received a $500 raise. Imagine that—$6200 a year. I loved to promote and sell. I won sales contests and was soon promoted to N-172, the largest store in Zanesville as co-manager. Another raise to $6700 a year. Kroger was good to me. I would work day and night. Sixty hours a week was about the pace, sometimes more. In late 1963, Kroger built a new store in Zanesville.

The manager of N-153 would be the new manager. N-153, the old store, was open, and I was offered the job. I had made store manager in little over a year. Captain Shafer had the same results in another town. Two Marines, what can I say. By then my eight years and the Marines were served. I was discharged but could be recalled up to age sixty.

Running any business was right up my alley. I had found my home and thought the salary of $7500 a year was humbling. The first thing I learned as a manager was *if it wasn't done, you did it.* Now I can work sometimes seventy hours a week. Whatever it took, I would do it.

N-153 was in downtown Zanesville. There were a lot of walking customers. The store was near the rundown, low-income section of town. One of N-153's biggest problems was "shrink" inventory loss. Shoplifting was a constant problem. I decided to crack down on shoplifting. My team united behind me, and my first year as manager we prosecuted over a hundred. The word was out.

Net profit improved. The net margin at that time was 1 to 2 percent of sales. Most people would never believe that. Our store hit 3 percent or better and finished the first year at 2.9 percent, net another $500 raise. Control is another way to produce a profit. Wages was the biggest expense.

You had guidelines to control the wage percent. It was hard to do in a union store. You had limits on how, when, and where you can place employees. Over time was to be avoided. Scheduling help was a major responsibility of management. Knowing when peak customer time was very important. It was almost impossible to get it right every week, so if you needed another register opened, someone to bag or carry out and there was no one, guess who, the manager would do all of these things and didn't hide in the office or back room on busy times.

There were some great hardworking people at Kroger. My endeavor at N-153 later produced four store managers and five department heads I recommended for promotion. We were a good team.

Now back to shoplifting. When I worked in the coal company stores, there were people who would steal. They would break into the store at night. My father took care of one break in as related with a Winchester 12 gauge, which solved that one. I still have that model 12.

When my mother became manager of a break-in, it occurred late at night. The store manager's house was next to the store. The store was equipped with a burglar alarm that ran into the house. My mother was a widow living alone. My sister was in Kentucky at Berea College going to school. My mother would have made a good female Marine! She got her loaded 38 special, and out the door she went. It was 2:30a.m. The nearest law enforcement was twenty miles away. She was the law enforcer.

She slipped in a back door, and before the intruder knew what happened, a pistol barrel was poked in the back of his neck with this red-headed crazy woman saying, "I will blow your head off. Do what I say." She marched him out the door to the store-front where there was a light. She alerted a neighbor who called the state police. About thirty minutes later, there were the state police with guns drawn. The thief was spread-eagled face down in the fresh gravel.

My mother knew one of the troopers. He said, "Mrs. Graham, you could have been killed."

She calmly said, "No, he could have been." The scared young man, about twenty-five, was glad to be put in the police car. "That crazy woman almost shot me." Once before I had seen her in action with a ball bat.

The two times I had ever been in a position to stop stealing was at the company store was seeing a miner's wife steal an item. I told Mr. Gibson. He went to the script window and withdrew enough script from her husband's wages. Quick justice.

Another time was in college as vice president of the student council. We suspected a student was stealing from other students at the dorm. We planted three marked bills for him to find. Sure enough, they disappeared.

Within an hour, he was off to take his girlfriend to the mov-ies. We followed him in with a local chief of police. We asked to see the bills he gave the cashier. Movies were 50¢, two tickets $1. It was the marked bill. He was arrested on the spot in the theater sitting beside his girlfriend. The next day he was expelled from college and sent home. Salem College had standards that were upheld.

Here I am again, dealing with thieves. There are two things I never tolerated—a liar or a thief. I had devised a system to handle shoplifters. Every employee watched. Notice their eyes; it was a dead giveaway. When a shoplifter was approached, he or she was very calmly asked to come to the office. I would push a button, and a buzzer would go off in the meat department. They would immediately call the police.

Two of us up front in the office had prepared a one-page confession the shoplifter was to sign. We tried to assure him or her to sign the paper. Most did, as they thought we would let them pay, and we would let them go. Usually by that time, we had defused the situation and were just talking to the shoplifter. The shoplifter did not see anyone calling the police. All at once a policeman, sometimes two, walked in the front door to the office beside the check lane said, "You're under arrest."

The shocked thief was placed in handcuffs and out the door to a police car parked in front of the door. Eighty percent of the time, we had a signed confession. Justice served. All the customers saw the arrest. The word spread quickly: "Go some other place to steal."

Shoplifters fall into several categories:

1. *Children.* Stealing candy, etc.—not to jail but must face mom and dad. In some cases, parents sent them there to steal.
2. *Transients.* Need food and wine, etc.
3. *Women.* Trying to save on a grocery bill. Beware of large purses and diaper bags.
4. *The true kleptomaniac.* Just stole.
5. *Men.* Tobacco and wine, etc.
6. *Those that stole to resell.* Cigarettes, etc.

About 95 percent of those I caught were prosecuted. Others were handled with special circumstance. One of those was the wife of a prominent man of the community and a fellow member of my church. I knew she had a problem. They did not need help with their grocery bill. She had two T-bone steaks and some expensive items from the health and beauty section. My first impulse was to call the police, but my background in college in the field of social work led me to believe she needed professional help. How was I to do this? Then it came to me: call Dr. Gordon the minister of our church. She agreed to see him and confessed what she had done. It was harder for her to do that than going to jail. He managed with her husband to get her help. However, she never shopped in my store again.

I could write five hundred pages of shoplifting experiences. Here are some that have to be told. One busy Friday, my co-manager spotted this old man stuffing things into a jacket pocket he was caring over his arm. He was approximately seventy-five to eighty years old and was heading out the door. We stopped him and asked him to come into the office. The usual buzzer to the meat department notified the police. This time it was not a uniformed policeman who came but a woman detective in street clothes. Her name was Bonnie Poland. She worked with Margaret in the prosecutor's office. The old man did not know who she was. Bonnie began asking him questions—what his name was, where he was going, etc. She picked up the suit jacket, it was heavy.

Both arms of the jacket had been sown shut, producing a great place for stolen items. Bonnie began taking items out, all food of some kind. He had enough to eat for two to three days. He was a transient. The last item she pulled out was a wash rag and a bar of used soap. She said, "What is this?"

The old man was getting irritated said, "It's soap. G—d—it, we West Virginians want to wash now and then."

Bonnie, my head checker, and I had to turn our heads to keep from laughing.

After he signed the confession, I called Bonnie over and said, "Take him to the city limits and let him go." After all I could not prosecute a fellow West Virginian who likes to wash once in a while. He made us laugh. Sometimes laughter is the best medicine.

Another time a man had a dozen eggs in a deep overcoat pocket. We were not sure what he had taken but knew he was trying to steal. As he was going out the door, we accidentally took a basket to block his path. He panicked and fell against the door. There were twelve scramble eggs going down his leg to his shoe. We wished him a good day and let him drip down the street.

One man drew a knife on me. No problem. I had experienced that in the coal camps. He went to jail. He was too drunk to use a knife. He was stealing wine.

One that stands out in my mind is a little boy about six to eight years old with his father reluctantly coming into the office in front of the check line. He was upset and crying. His dad, in and very rough voice, said, "Tell this man what you did."

In a trembling voice, he handed me a candy bar, crushed and mushy, he had stolen while in the store. He confessed and asked me not to send him to jail. I looked at dad who winked at me. After about a five-minute lecture on why you should not steal and how he had hurt his parents and he could not go through life taking things that did not belong to him, finally I said, "If I don't send you to jail, will you do what your mom and dad tell you so they can be proud of you?"

He shook his little head and wrapped his body around his dad's leg. Every little boy or girl should have a dad like that. Today I'm afraid in many cases a lawyer would be hired to sue.

TURNING POINT
TOUGH LOVE TOO WORKS—TRY IT

My parents did and this dad did. Little did I to know, I would have to practice tough love raising my son. He was about three at the time. Sometimes it hurts you more than it hurts your child. More on this later.

My second store to manage was N-157 in Columbus Ohio. One remarkable story regarding shoplifting. By this time, I had learned some tricks of the trade. I carried a nicely folded woman's handkerchief in my pocket and a man's comb. If we were watching a suspicious shopper and never saw them take anything, we would put the heat on them as they would usually go out a closed check line. Now you know why check lanes are blocked in stores.

A rather large black lady was acting suspicious. She had a large diaper bag pocketbook over her shoulder. As my dad would say, she was two-and-a-half ax handles across the rear bumper. She hurriedly went through the closed check lane with nothing visible.

I said in a loud voice, "Lady, did you lose this?" holding up the ladies' handkerchief.

She broke into a run, and in about two steps, this large object fell from between her legs. "Oh my God." Maybe she was pregnant, who could tell? She was not pregnant. It was a twenty-pound ham. The ham followed her out the door onto the street.

That woman can run, she still may be running. We retrieved the ham and all the customers who saw it could not believe how she was going to walk out of the store with that ham between her legs. Everyone started to laugh. The meat manager came up to take the ham back to the case. Later I went back, and there was that ham with a special label "Extra Smoked." He had also raised the price by seven cents per pound. He was a character. I could not argue with that, but I did not buy the ham.

N-157 was doing well with the third Kroger store now in Zanesville. Our profits were up, and I had a great team. I will never forget four of my employees who got their own store they deserved it.

A new general manager had come to Columbus. He reported to the vice president only. There were two layers of management between us. I was supervised by a zone manager who had nine stores. This general manager was outspoken and had come to Columbus to turn it upside down. He could have and might have been good, but company politics was not his thing.

My store N-153 was given an inspection by the new general manager as the ranking representative from the division. The next thing I knew, I was offered the store in Columbus, one of the biggest in the state. More money, prestige, and opportunity lay ahead. Mr. White, the general manager, told me I would be there a short time, and if I could increase sales and profits, my next move would be on his management team. This meant I could move up the corporate ladder and become a division vice president in time. *Wow*, $10,000 a year plus bonuses. Ten thousand dollars in 1965 was more than I had ever made in one year. I had a wife and son who would benefit. After talking it over with Margaret, I said yes, I would take it. What a wonderful wife I had; she did not want to move to Columbus but knew I wanted this opportunity.

Off to Columbus we had purchased a starter home in Zanesville, and the house would not sell at that time. So we had to rent in Columbus, living in a city that that size was an adjustment for this country boy. I did not know at the time I took this promotion that my zone manager's supervisor had one of his own men he wanted to move into that store.

The zone manager, Mr. Yarbrough, was not happy with the deal as I soon found out. He was about sixty and had been with Kroger for forty years. Here is a new divisional general manager going over his head taking his authority and power away. *Very quickly I came to a major turning point in my young life.* I was thirty years old and managing my second store, with seventy-seven employees and many older than me.

Nevertheless, I put myself into it, and the results were great—record sales and record profits. I was promoting sales, *Batman* was in, and I had a big *Batman* promotional. I was dressed as Batman, and my co-manager was Robin. We set record sales during this period as we used the Sam Walton model with customers. And I wanted their shopping to be happy and something to remember. I managed to get a photo-op with the Miss USA world of 1965. I still have our picture.

This packed the store. At last, I knew my calling *was sales, not law enforcement* officer. It was time to activate to the positive and eliminate the negative and spread joy to the affirmative and not mess with mister in between. A good song and a good plan for your life.

Our store won the top award for merchandise excellence. A large plaque was presented with all employee names, it could not have been better. I still have it in my office.

Miss USA World—Denise Blair 1966
Kroger N-157—Columbus, OH Micky Graham Store Manager

Then another hard learning experience. There is *hardball in company politics*. Mr. White, the general manager, was fired. He had stepped onto many toes. I hated that; he thought like me and expected everyone to give 110 percent.

My buffer of protection was gone. Mr. Yarbrough started putting the pressure on me. No one had ever pressured me to get the job done.

I became very much aware of managers in their early fifties getting the ax. We now had number crunchers in charge. A young man full of vim and vinegar would work for half as much and do what was asked of him. It was simple college educated arithmetic. Being in the $10,000 a year, this kid had replaced a fifty-year-old twenty- to twenty-five-year career man.

The store had just had the record sales and profits for the reporting period. I was very proud and had compensated all my associates. Mr. Yarbrough sat down with me to go over the report which had about forty columns of numbers with sales at the top and net profits at the bottom, over 4 percent—unheard of. I was expecting a raise. Instead he went to one item, "laundry" supplies, which was up slightly. He never mentioned the record sales and profits. He said, "What are you going to do about it?" Most of the laundry supplies were aprons and jackets used in the meat and perishables apartments.

I replied, shocked beyond belief, "I will take all the aprons away," and that made him mad.

I was never a good politician. Shortly after that, my grandfather died. I would have to miss one day of work to go to Southern West Virginia for the funeral. Mr. Yarbrough came in the same day for his store visit. I told him I had a death in the family, where it was, and I would have to miss a day's work.

His reply was "I buried a mother and a father and did not let it interfere with my work." Again, without thinking I said the first thing that came into my mind: "I am not a *damn bit surprised at that.*" *Turning point.* He never asked me who had died.

My grandfather was very special to me. I was going to the funeral. Only my mother was left, and I had moved her to Zanesville after the coal company store closed. She was lucky at her age to get a job managing the Plaid Stamp store.

After the funeral, I planned to return to Zanesville. The manager at the new Kroger store was being promoted. I asked for that store. My old boss was happy to have me back, but I had made a decision. *I will start my own business.* If I'm going to work between sixty and seventy hours a week, I'll do it for myself and family. It has to work, I found the competition is far less when you work for yourself. *You can accomplish anything if you believe in yourself.*

TURNING POINT
BE TRUE TO THYSELF

My years at Kroger gave me the opportunity to manage three stores, temporarily manage in another, co-manage in two, and short stints in others.

- Managed two stores in Zanesville, Ohio
- Managed one store in Columbus, Ohio
- Temporary manger in Glouster, Ohio
- Other stores in Cambridge and Martins Ferry, Ohio. At the coal camps in West Virginia, I worked at stores
- In Wyoming, Glover, Marianna
- In Wyoming County, West Virginia
- Dorothy and Marfork in Raleigh County, West Virginia
- Ronda, United Kayford, and Acme Kanawha County, West Virginia

Add the A&P Tea Company in Clarksburg in Harrison County, West Virginia to the list. I worked in sixteen different stores.

On my third store as manager in five years, I still owned a home in Zanesville. Up next to my best friend, I have ever had, Dana Bates. Dana's wife worked with Margaret and had the same birthday. We raised our kids together. Dana's girls made up for the girls I never had.

N-244 was a smaller store than the one in Columbus. It didn't matter I was preparing to be on my own.

Here I go again: "He can't hold a job." I had a lot to prove, Margaret believed in me, and that was all that mattered. I now know why the "garden of the Eden" was called paradise. There were no *relatives or in-laws*. Later I would gain approval from most of my relatives. But some would be envious and jealous as they would say, "I wish I could drive a New Lincoln and go on all those expensive trips."

I finally said, "I'm sorry too, I wish you could afford it," and I meant that. They worked regular hours, watched TV, etc. I worked all hours and did whatever it took to make it. I have *no patience with anyone who thinks the world owes them something.*

Before I leave the Kroger years, let me say to all those fine people I worked with: you helped me more than you'll ever know.

Going into business for myself. We made the move back to Zanesville for family reasons also. I moved my mother from West Virginia in 1965. The coal company store had closed, and she was alone for far too long. Alan was now five years old. I did not want to raise him in a large city like Columbus. I wanted him to grow up in a stable rural environment. He would have to learn the work ethic to be responsible. Our church in Zanesville was Market Street Baptist Church. The church had a great youth pro- gram. In a big city, your neighbors change constantly, and popula- tion growth brings more challenges.

Margaret was anxious to get back to her love of criminal law. A job at the prosecutor's office was waiting for her. She had achieved statewide recognition as a criminal paralegal secretary with the state prosecution association. Later she was named the outstanding secretary in the state by the state association of pros- ecuting attorneys. She also gave 110 percent to her work.

A lot of her work was secret. She was the "Della Street" to the prosecutor. Remember the Perry Mason TV series. People and investigations were something she did not share with anyone out- side of law enforcement. Many of her friends became my friends. The prosecutor's staff, sheriffs, detectives, deputies, etc. One of them was Barney Uffner, the sheriff. There will be a couple of stories about him later.

A *major turning point moving back to Zanesville.* We moved back to our modest home; we still could not sell. The renters had left their marks. It had to be repainted and refurbished. So much for renters. I did not learn this lesson well, as later rentals I owned had similar results.

Dana and Sue Bates were still there, and that close friendship remained to the present. Dana became the brother I never had. His kids were my kids also.

I am now the manager at N-244 Kroger in Zanesville. More old managers were being let go. Age had caught up. My boss was fired. It was time to go. *I was now thirty-three and had learned you must play politics to survive in the corporate world.* I loved *to sell and promote* and not to be the referee between the union and the company. It was time to consider *my first love, selling.* The *security of families.* If it had not been the small $5,000 insurance policy my dad had through group insurance, I would have had to drop out of college to help my mother and sister. The $5,000 was a lot of money in 1957. Insurance and investments fascinated me—this is what I wanted to do.

There were two ways to break into the business as an employee or as an independent contractor. I thought about going back to New York Life. I had done well in the short time I was with them. The usual companies like Metropolitan, Prudential, Western, and Southern were all available. There was always a turnover of agents.

It is a tough business. You have numbers on your head, produce, or starve out or get fired. As an employee agent, there are many reasons to consider—stability of income and a salary to start.

Opportunities for management—no, not again. I only *wanted to motivate myself.* Just maybe I could motivate people to buy insurance if they understand what it would do for them. The second way to go into business was as an independent contractor.

This was straight commission once it was paid for and put on the books. The process could take sometimes two to three months. I learned insurance companies hold onto the commissions as long as they could. *There was money to be made on the "float."*

One of the compelling reasons to enter business was I only saw one aggressive agent in the Zanesville area. Bob F. at Northwest Mutual.

He was on the board of directors at the local bank, knew who was applying for a loan, and had political connections. He had lawyers, doctors, and the white-collar market. No one called on me to sell me insurance. Why, I asked? I soon found out. Many of my friends had little or no life insurance. I would ask them, "Do you *own any life insurance?*"

About 90 percent would say, "Yes, I have it where I work."

I would reply, "*You plan to die while working? You are renting insurance.*"

A puzzled look would be on their face. "No." I found there were countless prospects.

It was time to educate myself. I read everything I could find about insurance and investments. It obvious to me that there were many products of security that the average family and small business could use if they only knew about them.

I did a lot of research and thought to make up my mind. The first decision was made. I wanted to be an independent contractor. I wanted to do it my way, as Frank Sinatra would say. *It would be my way or the highway.* It's a risky venture. Marine guts trumped brains and rational thinking. *I wanted opportunity, not security.* Security would come later as my dreams were fulfilled.

A successful agent could write his own paycheck. I had no desire to become a manager. I couldn't afford the pay cut. Some managers had quotas, agents had clients—big difference. There were good teachers and teachers who could not do anything else. As Winston Churchill said, if you fail at everything else, you can always teach school. From now on, I would do the teaching to better by clients. My eight years of school board will be covered later.

It took a while to come up to a turning point that caused me to be *the last of the poor boys.* Bedrock principles had been thrown out and replaced.

1. I wanted to sell not manage.
2. I wanted to be an independent contractor.
3. I wanted all forms of Insurance and investments I wanted mutual funds and other investments.

4. I would have all of Ohio to work with businesses and individuals.

Most of the major companies wanted you to be an employee agent. I had to find the right fit.

One day I saw a full-page ad in a magazine entitled "You can own part of America for as little as $20.00 a month." That appealed to me as most of my *poor boys* could do that. The company was called I.D.S Investors Diversified Service out of Minneapolis Minnesota. I had never heard of them but found two of their reps were working Zanesville and did not live there. Very interesting. I read the ad again, and they were looking for reps. I replied and mailed a tear-out sheet directly to Minneapolis. Hearing nothing by mail or phone, I figured they didn't want any more reps working in the Zanesville area.

I was wrong. There was a knock on my door one evening, and there stood a well-dressed man with a briefcase. He had just parked his car in my driveway, a new white Cadillac 1968 model, parked next to my 1967 VW beetle.

After two or three meetings, an interview with upper management people in Columbus, I said, "This is for me." *No salary, no paid expenses, no guarantees—just opportunity.* I proved to my family again that I had more guts than brains. It took about ten years to get the fear out of my system that they might be right.

Going with I. D S. was on automatic. I had to go thorough background check, had to be trained, and licensed not all only in life insurance but securities which required state and federal licensing. It took some time and study of about six months. This was hard to do and still manage the store.

Alan, my son, was now six and in school. I had saved a little money and withdrew my profit-sharing money as a manager. I was penalized heavily for early withdrawal. With that $2600 in hand, I began my sales career with I.D.S. in June 1968, ten years after graduating from college. Was this job number nine or ten? Nevertheless, I cannot hold a job, just ask relatives.

My last year with Kroger I made a little more than $13,000 which came up to about $4.12 per hour. Some of the union meat cutters made more. I was working between sixty and seventy hours a week. Let's see, sixty hours a week times fifty-two equals 3160 a year divided into 13,000 equals $4.12 an hour. I can do that mowing lawns if I had to. Also, the stores opened on Sunday now and every other Sunday I worked. I rotated with my co-manager; he was a family man also.

It was an easy decision to make. If I work as hard for myself as I do with Kroger, I have to make it. It worked, but where was my first sale coming from? I was about three months' living on the $2600 before I received a commission check for over $300.

Everyone was a prospect, but they had to be qualified. Some people live day-to-day and are not concerned about their financial future. I soon learned that at age sixty-five 90 percent or more people lived on social security or some other pension. Only 5 percent of those over fifty lived on the money they had saved or invested. *This was the secret to my type of selling.*

It's the same thing Willie Sutton, the infamous bank robber, knew. He was asked, "Why do you rob banks?"

"That's where the money is" was his simple answer. It worked for me.

I wanted to work with people who wanted to provide for themselves and their families. Soon, I realized most people wanted to do this. *I had found a home.* I could help them. One principle I carried for the next twenty-nine years: *if the sale does not make the client better, it's not a good sale.* It worked. Most of my competitors were still selling life insurance as a saving and investment. I did not. It was to create money when it was needed; it provided the umbrella over the family or business. You can be *premium poor, not insurance poor.*

Selling came easy as I was finally doing something in *social work* that was worthwhile. But I was selling and getting paid for it. About a year later, I bought my first Lincoln and had doubled my income I had made at Kroger, although I had expenses.

One Monday, I was in Columbus, Ohio. There was a division training meeting each Monday with IDS. Great Eastern shopping center had a Kroger store. I pulled into the parking to see an old Kroger friend. There was my old boss Mr. Yarbrough coming out of the store.

I recognized his Buick and pulled in behind it so he could not get out. He was irritated that I had him blocked. He got out of his car and walked toward the new Lincoln. I got out in my Lincoln new suit and said in my own way, "Mr. Yarbrough. *I want to shake your hand. If it had not been for you, I would still be with Kroger.*" With that, I got back into my Lincoln and drove away leaving an old, bald-headed man sweating in the sun. I owe him a lot. He helped me make one of the best decisions of my life. *I have to confess—I love this story.*

Our Texas home

Micky with "Chloe"
neighbors dog

CHAPTER 8

Building My Agency

For the next thirty years, I was my own man. Each year was an improvement financially except the "Jimmy Carter" area which I held my own. After six years with I.D.S., I realized I had to do the same thing over and over each year. I managed to make I.D.S.'s presidents club each year and was always a $1,000,000 producer. However, I was now approaching forty and can see I could not ever build a renewal residual income.

At this time, I was continuing my education enrolled in the CLU program with the American College of Bryn Mawr, Pennsylvania, the highest designation in life insurance. It stands for Chartered Life Underwriter. It requires time, sales experience, and passing ten examinations. It took me five years to do this. Most classes were held at Universities. I attended Ohio University, Ohio State, and West Virginia State for the final exam. I became the first CLU in Zanesville Ohio. Three other agents quickly completed their designation. I later completed two other designations—CHFC (Chartered Financial Consultant) and LUTCF (Life Underwriter Training Class Fellow), all through the American College and the National Association of Life Underwriters.

It was time to grow in the insurance business. I wanted to expand into all lines of insurance. This opportune came in my CLU classes at Ohio University. I met Dick Moore, who was a manager for Nationwide Insurance Office in Columbus, Ohio, fifty miles away.

I had to start all over again building a client base. But now I could serve all the needs of individuals and businesses. Zanesville, Ohio was not a growing area. In order to sell automobile, home, and business insurance, I had to compete with agents and agencies that had my prospects as customers.

More people were moving out rather than into the Zanesville area.

It became clear to me, I would do what was best for my clients, not what most of my competition did. I looked at all my clients' insurance needs. My goal was to become their adviser and cover them properly at the lowest possible cost. All sales interviews would follow this procedure. Client first, company second, and me third.

1. What it is best for the client?
2. The insurance company comes in second and I as an agent come last.
3. Being last in this case is best.

I never tried to put *commissions above the needs of the client* or insurance company. After all, the agent represents both client and company.

I was now selling all types of insurance—mutual funds, annuities, pensions, IRAs, profit sharing, pension plans, and group insurance. This was not easy to do. I had to have a staff to provide good customer service. Making the right decision on people has been the turning points in my life.

Martha Ross became the best *personal decision of my career.* She became my right arm, and we built the agency together for the next twenty-three years. She helped me make it happen. I had the best *mother, wife, and Martha Ross. She was my "mastermind"* person, as described by Napoleon Hill and his book *Think and Grow Rich*.

For the next twenty-three years, our agency grew and grew, expanding in offices in two counties of Ohio's poverty areas. One simple principle was followed; *do what the competition does not or will not do*, and you will succeed. Working six days a week sixty to seventy hours will bring success in anything *you believe in*. I was on a mission.

Martha Ross "my right arm"

Featured Speaker—Micky Graham Agent- Zanesville, Ohio

PENNSYLVANIA FARMERS' ASSOCIATION
AND
NATIONWIDE INSURANCE COMPANIES

Together, serving the needs of Pennsylvania's Farm Families

SPECIAL GUESTS

Representing Nationwide's Board of Directors

Henry S. Halloway
Chairman of the Board, Nationwide Mutual Fire Insurance
Board Sponsor Committee Member

Charles L. Fuellgraf, Jr.
Chairman of the Board, Nationwide Development Company and Nationwide
Communications, Inc.

Representing Nationwide's Home Office, Columbus, Ohio

| **Patrick S. Roberts** | **Tom G. Brunk** |
| V.P., Sponsor/Endorsor Relations | Photo Mgr., Public Relations |

James R. Gildea
Director, Special Services

Featured Speaker
Mickey Graham
Agent, Zanesville, Ohio

NATIONWIDE INSURANCE ENTERPRISE

HOME OFFICE ONE NATIONWIDE PLAZA, COLUMBUS, OHIO 43216-2220

D. RICHARD McPHERSON, CLU
President and Chief Executive Officer

TELEPHONE 614/249-4631
FAX 614/249-9711

February 1, 1994

Mr. Alfred Graham
P. O. Box 70
Zanesville, OH 43702

Dear Micky:

Congratulations on qualifying for MDRT!!

This is certainly a prestigious accomplishment that brings broad recognition, not only across the Enterprise, but across the industry as a true professional. Most importantly, your customers value your professionalism as you provide them financial security and peace of mind. As you know, you are among Nationwide's most elite group and I want to salute you for that.

Once again Micky, congratulations on a job well done. I look forward to offering my congratulations to you in person here in Columbus in April.

Sincerely,

Dick

DRM/mj

Great job. Two years in a row with all the challenges you carry.

cc: Jerry Daughtry

Nationwide Mutual Insurance • Nationwide Mutual Fire Insurance • Nationwide Life Insurance • Nationwide Insurance Companies
Colonial Insurance • Farmland Insurance • Financial Horizons Life • GatesMcDonald • National Casualty Insurance
Nationwide Agribusiness Insurance • Nationwide Communications • Nationwide Financial Services • Nationwide General Insurance
Neckura Insurance Companies (Germany) • PEBSCO • Scottsdale Insurance • West Coast Life Insurance

---

Industry awards were many. I qualified for Nationwide's president's club award fourteen times a record which still stands in the Zanesville area. With six presidential awards from IDS, I made it twenty years. Some of those accomplishments included the Million Dollar Round Table, National Sales Achievement Award, and National Quality Award by the National Association of Life Underwriters. The service award winner twice for community service.

My first office—Martha Ross and Micky Graham 1973

- I was the first agent for Nationwide in Ohio to sell two million dollars in life insurance in one year
- Company leader in annuity sales
- Agent of the year for my region eight times
- Awards for quality loss ratios in auto and fire
- President of the Zanesville Life Underwriters Association

- National president of the Nationwide agent association
- Elected to two-to-four-year terms on the local school board
- Served eight years on the county children's services board, appointed by the county commissioner
- Served as the official adviser for all areas of insurance for Muskingum County, Ohio. This was a non-compete position. This gave me an opportunity to use my knowledge and experience. The result was writing bid specifications for all of the county's insurance. Costs were lowered significantly and coverage was improved. They were still carrying $50 deductible collision on all their vehicles. Several thousand dollars were saved for the taxpayers.

I was involved in providing insurance to school districts at this time. Nationwide became available for property and casualty insurance for schools. The result was savings for the taxpayer and improving coverage of the schools.

Over the years, I taught many insurance classes and helped train agents and new employees. It was a wonderful rewarding career. Many times I went to the funeral home for a client I had insured. I could say more than "I'm sorry," but I could deliver a check for the life insurance and advise the heirs of their options.

One death claim stands out in my mind. I had sold a rather large policy to the president of one of my commercial accounts. He was forty-six years old and held a PhD degree was a very intelligent client. I encouraged him to set up an irrevocable life insurance trust and let the trust own the policy. The trust was managed by his local bank.

He was a pilot and owned his own plane. Being headstrong, he took off one Saturday morning in a heavy fog. He became disoriented and crashed into a tree. As usual, I went to the funeral and offered my condolences to the widow. I said I was very sorry about Phil.

She looked me in the eye and said, "You should not be sorry. He did not believe in life insurance, you are the only one that ever sold him." I had made a dear friend. Her life would be secure financially. This was the reason I loved the life insurance business. I could help my clients and their families when this would happen. No one else could say anything, but I'm sorry. I could say, "I am sorry but will be delivering a check to you and be there to advise you." *This is the greatest reward a life insurance agent can have.*

There are many rewards for achievement in sales. I was fortunate to qualify for great convention trips. Memories of those trips and the people I met changed my life forever. Some of those include:

- Hawaii (four times)
- San Diego, California—Twin Towers
- The Broadmoor, Colorado Springs, Colorado (twice)
- Seattle, Washington—The Space Needle
- The Greenbrier Resort—W.V. (three times)
- Toronto, Canada
- Myrtle Beach, South Carolina (three times)
- Hilton Head, South Carolina (two times)
- The Concord, New York
- San Francisco, California
- French Lick Resort, Indiana
- Amelia Island
- Puerto Rico Ceroman Beach Hotel
- Saint Thomas and the Virgin Islands
- Cayman Islands
- Columbus, Cleveland, Ohio
- University of Michigan
- New Orleans Louisiana
- Orlando, Florida—The "Peabody" Hotel
- Palm Springs, California—The Canyon Hotel
- Hershey, Pennsylvania—Convention Center
- Atlantic City, New Jersey

- Innisbrook Resort—Florida
- Las Vegas, Nevada
- Reno, Nevada

On many of these trips, I was a speaker and participated in panels and put on seminars on many areas of sales and motivation. It was my great honor to rub elbows with many nationally known personalities. There's a partial list of those I had dinner with, shook hands, or had a conversation I will relate stories on some.

H. Row "Big Chief" Bartel—then mayor of Kansas City Missouri. He brought pro football to Kansas City and was a close friend and adviser to Harry Truman.

The Blue Angels 1957, Kansas City, Missouri.

Napoleon Hill—famous author and motivator. His book, *Think and Grow Rich,* was the roadmap for my life and career. I was privileged to introduce him as a commencement speaker at Salem College, West Virginia in 1957, being president of my senior class. After his address, we went backstage. Dr. Hill asked me what I was going to do with my life. At age twenty-three, I had never thought about the life of fifty or sixty more years. At that point, Dr. Hill gave me a hardbound, autographed copy of his book *Think and Grow Rich.* He said, "This book will tell you how to accomplish good thing and in anything you undertake." *Wow,* was he right. He was over eighty year of age. I still have his book, and outside of the Bible, I think it was the greatest book ever written.

A few years ago, I was offered fifteen hundred dollars for his autographed copy. I will never sell it, I will pass it down. During the past fifty years, I have bought many copies, given them to people who can dream and have that *"fire in the belly."* It worked for me.

I also met Branch Rickey of the old Brooklyn Dodgers who brought Jackie Robinson into professional baseball. He also had a tremendous effect on my life.

About the same time, one of my college professors and vice president at Salem college came into my life. Cecil H. Underwood was his name. He was a conservative republican and so was I.

Republicans were a species almost extinct in 1956 West Virginia. Cecil was elected to the state legislature, and in 1956 he ran for governor. I formed *"Students for Underwood"* in West Virginia. We work hard for him and sold our blood to donate to his campaign. *We made national headlines.* It was well worth it; he was elected in 1956 as the youngest governor in history at the age of thirty-four. The later became the oldest man elected governor in West Virginia. He was instrumental in introducing me to the insurance business.

During a convention at the Peabody Hotel in Orlando, Florida many years later, I met the famous *"Rice Twins."* They were dwarfs twenty-six-inches tall. I was one of the speakers, and they followed me on stage. As I went backstage, they looked up at me and John said, "You're pretty good." He then asked me how much I got paid for the speech.

I said, "I did it for my company."

Then he said, "We get $10,000," and walked past me to the speaker stand. Guess who the dwarf was and who was standing tall? We became good friends, and I still have my picture made with them. I was on my knees and still taller. Their story is legend. Johnny Carson had them on his show many times. Their motto was "Think big"—good advice for anyone. Never be satisfied with your comfort zone. "I think big." *I did. It paid off.*

Nationwide's man of the year. Also pictured in US News Week, US News Report and US News and World Report

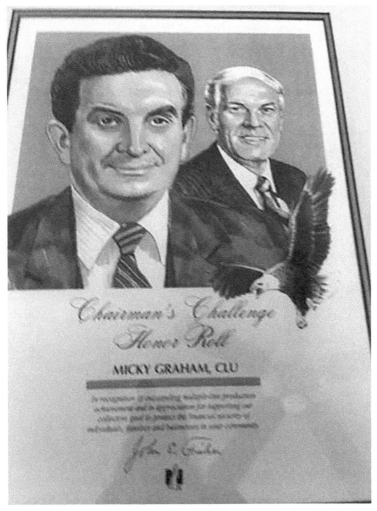

Micky Graham pictured with John Fisher Chairman
of the Board for Nationwide Insurance

The famous Rice twins

Micky Graham with the Rice twins

Ninety-nine percent of everything I did in life came from other people—their ideas, examples, and habits. I associated with the winners and achievers. *They will pull you up the losers in life will pull you down.* Others had impressed me, and many more were focused and goal-oriented. Here are some people I met who gave me challenges.

Ben Fieldman. New York Life agent who sold more life insurance than many companies combined. He had his own plane and doctors to do exams. He sold in many states.

Mom meeting Willard Scott

Willard Scott. NBC weatherman. I met him in Hawaii; he was a featured speaker. My mother went with me and had to be in a wheelchair. She and I went in early so she would have a front row seats in the handicap section. We were one of the first ones in the auditorium. In walked Willard Scott. He made a beeline to my mother and made her feel like the most important person he had ever met.

Great people are great alone or in a crowd. I treasure that picture with him hugging my mother. She passed away a year later. I could write a book on the positive effects that she had on me including getting a willow switch taken to my bare legs for wearing my school shoes in the creek in 1939. The Depression was still on. I learned not to waste but to appreciate everything in life.

Mike K. Coach K of the Duke Blue Devils basketball fame was a keynote speaker at another convention in Hawaii as a top agent. I was privileged to sit next to him for the formal banquet. Duke had just won a national championship. As we were eating side by side, I asked him about the high pressure in that final game.

Without missing a bite, he said, "Once you had played for Bobby Knight, there is no more pressure." He played for Coach

Knight at Army. Lesson learned and learn well. I met or had dinner with other famous coaches and athletes.

Lou Holtz. Football coach. I always asked questions. I wanted to learn from everyone. I asked Coach Holtz why he did not go to Alabama when Coach Bear Bryant died. He looked me right in the eye and said, *"Man, they can't spell football in Alabama."* Maybe that is the reason he went to Notre Dame. I adopted Lou Holtz's famous WIN philosophy. It is simply do what *is important now*. WIN.

Roger Staubach. The famous Heisman trophy winner and quarterback of the Dallas cowboys impressed me with his quiet example and character of his life. I had dinner with him, and he gave me an autographed football.

Archie Griffin. The only two-time Heisman trophy winner was a real Christian believer. He was the exact opposite of most football players. He was humble and had a purpose for his life. I was privileged to introduce him as a speaker for my church's 150th year anniversary. He gave an excellent message with his well-worn Bible in his hand.

ARCHIE GRIFFIN

I have met many elected politicians over the years. The list is as follows:

Senator Joseph McCarthy. I was fourteen or fifteen at the time. This was in the late '40s. My father took me to hear him speak in Charleston, West Virginia. He was later censored by the Senate for his extreme view. He predicted what was going on in American universities. The communists and socialists couldn't win at the ballot box but could infiltrate our schools and universities and win the battle of the minds. His predictions are coming true. He was years ahead of his time.

Governor John Kasich of Ohio. I met him at a political rally. He looked me straight in the eye as he shook my hand and answered my question. No nonsense, he believes in what he says. I would have voted for him for president. Not so sure now.

President Jerry Ford. I did not get to talk to him but almost walked into him at the Canyon Resort in Palm Springs, California. The Secret Service people stopped me in my tracks. No wonder he was an alumni at the University of Michigan and an Eagle

Scout. He was an all-American center. He had broad shoulders and looked like a real leader.

Others I heard or saw in person were Harold Stassen, who ran for president several times, Nelson Rockefeller, and Dan Quayle, who were both Vice Presidents.

I have been honored and privileged to meet many people who are not famous but left a long impression on me. Donna Harvey, Gladys Gray, Estel Morgan, Clifford Hanson, K. Duane Hurley, William Rollins, Henry Ash, and Clem Clower were all educators that put up with me and motivated me. One school principal, Mr. Curtis, applied the "board of education" which was a large coal mine bank belt to my seat of learning that helped me make good decisions.

Donna Jean Harvey had me in the second grade at Laurel Branch School near Clearfork, West Virginia in 1941. It was a one-room school. All eight grades, a burnside stove, a water bucket and dipper, and two paths that led to the restrooms. She told me I should go to college. No one else ever told me that. It was hard to tell a head-strong mischievous boy anything. Anyway, thirteen years later, I did go to college with no loans and no one to pay my way. What she said in 1941 stayed with me.

Mickey Rooney was starring in a musical play in Columbus Ohio. He autographed my program. I told him my name was Micky. He stopped instantly and looked me in the eye and said, "God help you, I've been married six times." God did help me; I have had two wonderful wives.

Bob Hope. Met Bob Hope at a banquet in Columbus Ohio. I was surprised that he was only five-feet-six-inches tall but a powerful influence on everyone he met. I also saw his home in Palm Springs, California. His dining room could seat three hundred people.

I accomplished everything in my career that was possible to do. It was over; time to smell the roses. Then the unexpected happened. Margaret developed cancer and diabetes. We would spend the next five years of our life in our airstream, seeing the country.

I have many wonderful memories. I lost her in 2001. She beat the cancer but not the diabetes.

Alan graduated from Ohio University, summa cum laude, and has been successful as a software engineer. I have three grandchildren. Wesley, the eldest, also a graduate of Ohio University as a mechanical engineer. Laura has a PhD from the University of Kentucky. She also has a BA degree in chemistry and a BA in math from Miami University. Zack has a bachelor's degree from Ohio University and an MBA from the Fisher school, Ohio State University. Very proud of them all. Yes, a Dr. Laura in the family.

Just as I thought my life was over in 2001, I accidentally ran into my heartthrob from Pineville High School, Betty. She had been a widow for ten years. Neither of us ever planned to get married again. I was living in Florida, she was still in Pineville, West Virginia.

My Aunt Allie turned ninety in 2001. I drove back to West Virginia to be at her birthday party. She helped raise me. I was very close to her.

I still had another Aunt Helen who lived close by. Couldn't visit one without visiting the other. Upon arriving at her house, she was on the telephone. Waiting for her to finish, I sat down. She did not hang up and said, "Here, come talk to Betty."

"Betty who?" I asked.

"Betty Beavers." Betty's daughter married my AUNT Helen's son. Her name was Charlene. I had met her at family reunions and knew her mother was Betty Jane Taybor. I took the phone and talked with Betty whom I had not seen or spoken to in fifty-two years. Betty knew I had been through a rough time dealing with the slow death of a loved one. To make a long story short, she said, "If you need to talk, here is my phone number."

Micky and Betty Graham

I wrote her phone number in my checkbook and exchanged reminisces of the past. I was heading back to Florida in my motor home. Over a month later, one night at about 9:00p.m., I was balancing my checkbook and there was Betty's number. Needing to talk to someone, I dialed the number. We talked briefly, I realized she had company, and ended the conversation. Nearly two hours later, Betty called me back and said she was not through talking to me. This began a two to three times a week phone conversation. I found out later her boyfriend was there the first time I called. The calls became more frequent and longer. I had to change my phone system to reduce the bill. A new life was beginning for both of us.

This is very different at age sixty-seven than at seventeen. We had to meet. Off to West Virginia again. However, we had talked marriage over the phone and agreed to get married. She told me she weighed 250 pounds, was now a blond, and not a redhead.

The rest is history. We're still talking after seventeen happy years. Margy, my first wife, and I decided to get married on our second date. Betty and I decided over the telephone. When you know, you know. Betty's ex-boyfriend said Betty went berserk when she talked to that Micky "feller,"

Two entirely different marriages, both winners. I have been blessed having too great wives; many men have not had one good marriage. Now I know why I had success in selling. I convinced one woman to marry me on the second date, and the other over the phone. That's called closing the sale. It's time to retire while I am batting a thousand. Can anyone top that in marriage?

Footnote: Betty had two sisters who married second cousins of mine. Her mother was a redhead, so was mine. They look alike and had to know each other.

Both of our fathers had jet black hair. We both have a Cherokee Indian ancestry. I believed in the power of prayer and feel the supreme power knowing your heart and needs. He brought Betty and I together.

We have been fortunate to share children and grandchildren and great grandchildren and friends for the last fifteen years. At this point, we have two daughters, one son, nine grandchildren, and seventeen great-grandchildren, and they still keep coming. Somebody close the door. We are overrun with relatives, we love it.

Betty and I continued to travel as Margy and I did. We made all fifty states—Canada, Mexico, many of the islands, and hope to do a few more. The motor homes are now history, but the memories are forever. Spending two months in the Canadian Rockies and Alaska was a dream come true. Yes, I am blessed and give praise to God. He has looked after me all my life.

There's more to life than making money. Life is an adventure. We came from some place and are going someplace. There is a beginning and an end. How you live this adventure is your choice. *Everyone must develop a master plan for his or her life.* Goals should be set, reviewed, worked, and accomplished. When one goal is met, another should be set. *Never be content doing nothing.*

Life is not complete unless you are giving back to others and hopefully making the world around you a little better than you found it.

Being active in my church began in 1955. As a college student, I taught Sunday school for a junior high group. My future brother-in-law, one of the students, was ornery then and still is at age seventy-one. I would work with the church Boy Scout Troop.

After moving to Zanesville Ohio in 1959, we joined the Market Street Baptist Church. Margy and I both became active, both Sunday school teachers. We enjoyed working with young people and became very close to the high school kids. All the girls were my girls, and the boys were adopted by Margy. We could always tell when one of the kids was rebelling at home with mom or dad. They would sit with us during church. One Sunday, Lora sat next to me she was seventeen or eighteen at the time. After church, her mother said to me, "*Your daughter might listen to you. Straighten her out.*" I loved her and still hear from her at Christmas. She now has raised five children in the church—mission accomplished.

Over the years at Market Street, we made many lifelong friendships and raised our children together. Don Cain, choir director, and his wife Bonnie had four children, including twin boys, my son Alan's age. Bonnie is gone, but Don lives in Florida with me in the same retirement resort. We have been friends for fifty-nine years. Sadly, Don passed away in 2018.

I served on the church board and as the church moderator. Those were good years. When Margy died, her funeral was at Market Street. During the thirty-eight days she lay in hospice, church members took turns being there for me. Great people, great friends. Rev. Scott Johnson was a gifted messenger of God.

When Betty and I got married, we went back to Market Streets and were married at 8:00 a.m. and introduced to a shocked church at 10:00 a.m.

Back in Florida, we went to a start-up Baptist church which met in the minister's home and a vacant store front. As usual, I got drafted to head the search committee for a church building. In a surprise move, the committee delegated me to handle the entire transaction. I found a church in town that was closing. Miraculously, we secured enough money to persuade a local bank to finance it. The church has since paid off the debit and is still growing. I had the great honor of being the first *ordained deacon* of the church. In Texas, we belonged to another large Southern Baptist church.

Now at Travelers Rest Resort, we have a strong church association. Church starts November and runs until after Easter. A retired minister serves as chaplain. The church is unique. Most are snowbirds from twenty or thirty states and Canada. Participants range from Catholics, Baptists, Methodists, Presbyterians, and all other denominations, with a few heathens like Don Cain and I. Over the years, I have served as treasurer and general chairman.

Outside the church, I have been involved in many projects—raising money for battered women, the needy, blood drives, as other church evangelism.

In 1979, I was asked to attend a Gideon International meeting in Zanesville. Staying in hotels and being inducted into the Marine Corp, I knew about the Gideon Bibles but nothing about the Gideons. I soon became involved and developed into a camp officer and Gideon lay speaker. During the last thirty-eight years, I have given the Gideon message in many churches who help finance this great mission. For those who are not familiar with the Gideons, they are a Christian business and professional men with their wives who are members of the Gideon's Auxiliary.

We pay all expenses of our ministry. Money is given by churches and individuals who distribute Bibles, all over the world and in over two hundred countries. Many Gideons do this at the risk of their own lives in foreign lands. It has been my great privilege to visit jails and penitentiaries to give testaments to inmates. And when we were allowed to give fifth graders in public schools, I was honored to have that opportunity. At one time, Gideons were not allowed to distribute Bibles in communist Russia. After President Reagan helped bring down the Berlin wall and the USSR was broken up, almost immediately Gideon camps started up in Russia.

Today, Russian Gideons can go into Russian schools. Here in the United States, Gideons are being pushed out in the name of separation of church and state. Our schools and country are now seeing the result. "Wake up America," everything else is in the schools but God's Word. Some other activities played major roles in my life.

The food stamp debacle. During President Carter's administration, 1976 to 1980, a major effort started to put anyone on food stamps whether they wanted them or not. In Zanesville, signs sprang up to encourage people to sign up. Some of my clients told me people were knocking on their doors, encouraging them to apply for food stamps. One older widow was insulted. She could live without them but did qualify for them. Families were supposed to take care of their own, not the federal government. It's a matter of choice and pride. *Freedom is not for sale.*

Something inside me responded to this. My first reaction was to write a letter to the local newspaper. It was printed. My letter stated that the needy need assistance, but this approach to organized "sign up" was not good for the taxpayers or recipients. The result would be total dependency on government. This has happened to a large segment of our population. *Many have lost their motivation and are satisfied with a lower comfort level.* This is our great country being destroyed, and it can lead to its demise. An entitlement society will greatly *reduce poor boys and motivation.* This may be the end of the poor boys like me.

My phone started ringing. People agreed with my letter. Local politicians called. A committee was formed and once again, I was on my own "white horse" leading the charge. *The Lone Ranger was my childhood hero.* The local media covered the committee uproar. We planned a large rally at the fairgrounds.

Donations came in. It was like a snowball. Far away, papers and TV News were starting to cover what we were doing. Thousands of signatures were obtained opposing the methods of the Carter administration. The signs on the telephone poles came down. Going door to door to sign up people stopped. A prominent local successful businessman gave me a blank check to cover our expenses.

We drew a packed fairground. Several local politicians, civic groups, and organizations joined in. *The Paul Harvey radio show picked up the fight.* Washington representatives from the department of agriculture came to Zanesville to interview me. Somebody listened.

Ronald Reagan became president, and "workfare for food stamps" was instituted. The Apostle Paul faced the same problem in the early church at Thessalonica. Many of their members quit working, thinking the second coming was eminent. In 2 Thessalonians, Chapter 3, verse 10 says it well: *"Let him who will not work let him not eat."* It would still work today, if we were not intent on the redistribution of income and trying to make us all socialists. We need safety nets for those that are unable to work, poor health, etc., but we don't need Santa Claus out of Washington to solve our local problems. That's up to us. *When we make everyone equal, there will be no more "poor boys" who want to do better. When we destroy our motivation, we destroy ourselves.* We must not let that happen.

I would do it all over again. But at eighty-four, someone of younger age must follow with a "fire in his or her belly," stand up, and be counted. Creeping socialism will destroy motivation in time for most people.

Micky Graham presenting an award to
the Franklin School District

Serving on the school board. In 1975, I was elected for a four-year term on the Franklin local school board in Muskingum County, Ohio.

I was reelected in 1979 until 1983. I had always been interested in government and political affairs. Prior to this time, I was president of the local PTA. My son Alan was in junior high, and we were involved in many school projects.

My insurance business was rapidly growing and finding time for civic duty was difficult. An event with my son opened my eyes to reality. He was thirteen and tall as I am—a big boy for his age. He came home from school one day and refused to do something his mother and I told him to do. Looking right into my eye, he said, "Ms. Forsythe told the class they can call children's services if their parents spanked them."

I remember what my father did when I challenged him as a teenager. I questioned him why I should do whatever it was about and said, "Let's talk about it." The next thing I knew, my dad's arm had me by the shirt neck and held me off the ground with one hand. He calmly said, "Go ahead and talk." I could hardly breathe, let alone talk. The conversation was over. I did what I was told.

The situation was different with Alan. He was as big as I was. There was no willow switch nearby, but there were my trousers support belt which was applied to his intellectual seat of knowledge. It only lasted a few seconds; I made my point. I then pointed to the phone and said, "Go ahead and call 'children's services.'" The very surprised teenager went back to the drawing board.

Ms. Forsythe was a new teacher just out of college, full of liberal philosophy and theory. At this point, I became concerned over what Alan had begun to tell me about school. He complained about drugs. He said marijuana was smoked in the boys' restroom, and the smoke was thick. I could not believe that. So it was time to visit the school, and the first step was to pay my respects to Ms. Forsythe and hear her side of the story. It was an open house for parents to visit the classrooms.

Armed with dress suit and tie with briefcase under my arm, I approached Alan's room. I was too late. A farm mother had Ms. Forsyth against the wall with her finger almost up her nose. The conversation was loud and not academic. This lady came from a local farm family that were grain farmers. She had, no doubt, had a lot of corn to eat. As my dad would say, two ax handles across the rear. I actually felt sorry for Ms. Forsythe. Mission accomplished, Ms. Forsyth got the message.

There were many good teachers in Franklin and some not so good and some who should be in an atmosphere that recognizes their incompetence. A job in Washington would master talents in my opinion. Most districts and the entire secondary education system is like this.

This brought back memories of my brief two-year career as a teacher—too much being politically correct, compromising standards, poor teachers' pay, and too much emphasis on athletics.

My first school board meeting set the tone. The board met at the high school. I arrived early with my suit and briefcase. There were five board members, treasurer superintendent, and assistant superintendent with chairs around in a large rectangular table. I sat down and waited. The other board members began arriving. One, who was the local mortician and also owned a large furniture store, had been on the board many years. "My *chair*! You are sitting in my chair!"

What does any dumb ignorant West Virginia hillbilly do? I got up too, turned the chair upside down, and said, "I didn't see your name on it."

This brought a chuckle from other board members. He sat red-faced in another chair. We became friends later. He too admired my spunk. Off to a great start. I later was elected president of the board and was named to the all Ohio school board.

Most school districts then and now are primarily concerned about budgets, finance, and personnel. Franklin was no different. This was a very rural school district. The bus routes covered over twenty-seven hundred miles a day on mostly back roads. The area was decreasing in population. Unemployment was high in that part of Ohio. Most graduates did not go to college but worked the same as their parents or moved on and left the area.

Sports dominated every aspect of the school's board meeting. Meetings were also dominated about sport issues. Replacing the coaches and who is satisfied with what the coaches did or did not do.

Too much mass communicating. Board members of any organization are to set policy and see that it is carried out. *Everyone who wants to run everything in any organization will harm that organization and what it is trying to accomplish. Micromanaging is not for the board of directors, setting policy is.*

One time after three hours of discussing the basketball coach and team problems, I had had enough. I put a motion on the floor to eliminate "basketball" in the school program. It failed for lack of a second but moved the meeting on to another subject. It made the board think about priorities.

Academics were always last on the agenda instead of being first. Serving eight years was informative, rewarding, and an educational experience.

To me, fiscal responsibility of our tax money was very important. I studied the financial report and questioned everything I did not understand. The first year for me, it looked like the district would have a surplus carry over into the next year. Great, right? No!

The superintendent said the district had to spend most of it before December 31 or we would lose X amount of dollars next year in state and federal aid. So much for reducing taxes. Living on a budget is mandatory for most American families. At least it used to be. This principle should be emphasized and enforced from the local school district, the courthouse, the state, and federal governments. There is plenty of tax money that is not being spent wisely.

Some of my experiences are as follows: consolidation with another small district. Installation of a compression gas system to power our many school buses. The savings paid the cost in the first year.

Opening the board meetings with a prayer. I was very involved in opening the school board meetings with a prayer and a pledge of allegiance. We were told we would be sued. Another board member said, "Sue us." Again, stand up and be counted. Publishing sick days of employees on the bulletin board in the school office and teachers' lounge reduced sick days. Most say 90 percent were always sick on Monday or Friday. Tuesday, Wednesday, and Thursday, most employees got better. Doing a study of bus mileage by each bus provided interesting information on gas mileage. Many buses were taken home by the driver as it was cheaper than bringing it to the central garage and more convenient to the larger rural area. *Several of the buses in this category got very poor gas mileage.* A little investigation revealed several farm tractors and lawnmowers might have been sucking on the public teat. We published those numbers, and surprisingly those buses started getting better gas mileage.

At that time, the district paid 100 percent of the health insurance on the employees and their families. I volunteered to look into all the districts' insurance. This was my expertise. Many of the teachers had spouses who taught in another district who had similar plans. This brought in problems of primary and secondary insurance. We were paying for coverage that would never be needed or used.

When a small premium for dependent coverage was charged back to the employee, most of the double dipping stopped. The employees were ahead of the administration and school board.

This is what is going on in many of our federal and state entitlement programs. Many people soon learn how to work the system. Again, motivation in the wrong direction. *They accepted a lower, comfort level because it's easier.*

It has never been my motivation to micromanage on any board I served. I will mention three other boards two of those were for profit corporations.

Getting back to the school board. There were two instances where I acted individually to correct the situation that was unacceptable in my view. The first was one of the "warming oven" story. From time to time, I would visit a school unannounced to learn and observe. The Chandlesville Elementary was a small school in the district. The hot lunch program was run by two employees who were mother and granddaughter. This was rural farm country. Farm women serve hot food and have pride in cooking—at least it used to be.

This day I arrived at lunchtime. Due to the limited seating, students were served in shifts. The first shift always got hot food. Sometimes the second shift had food that had cooled. Today the menu was pizza. I can see the stress on the gray-haired grandma serving the cold pizza. She was upset. I asked her if I could help. she said there were no warming ovens for the kids' food.

I asked, "Have you requested them?"

"Yes, I was told there was no money in the budget." It so happened the next board meeting was two days away. I had planned to bring up this item for discussion. As fate would dictate, arriving at the new board office, I saw that the parking lots had been paved and several improvements to the old house we had converted into the office. At that time, any purchase over $5000 had to be approved. I knew it was more than $5000 had been spent on asphalt in that parking lot.

I was the first board member there. The superintendent parked his car beside mine and asked me what I thought of the fine paving job. I told him it was great, but I would not bring up the failure of getting board approval if Chandlesville school would suddenly get warming ovens. Guess what, the warming oven arrived before the week ended. I went back to the Chandlesville school to see a smiling cook. We were both happy, and so were the kids. More than one way to "skin a cat."

Another incident involved high school graduation. Being president of the board, it was my privilege and honor to present the diploma to each senior. This was my first time doing this. The event was held at the football stadium.

As the line started and names were called, I noticed the first boy had no socks or shoes. Then I realized he had no pants, just a graduation gown and cap. Seems most of the boys were robed only. Decision time.

Do I stop the line or ignore it? I chose to ignore it and finish the ceremonies. It did not take me long to corner the superintendent and the high school principal after the ceremonies. The explanation I got was that boys will be boys, and they did not want to upset the ceremony and the several hundred parents and friends. I was told "there is nothing they could do" about it. I was as "ornery as any boy growing up." I still remember Mr. Curtis the principal in high school and his uplifting belt experience. I agreed with the superintendent and principal that if there was nothing they could do, *maybe a new superintendent and principal could solve the problem.* Next year, the problem had been solved. Old parable of mine: meetings don't solve problems, people one-on-one solves problems and get results.

Eight years is a long time, and in my opinion, no one should hold office longer. Often they become the problem and no longer are fit to meet the needs and objectives of the electorate. It was a great experience for me. I had been full circle from student, college graduate, PTA, teacher, coach and board member, and parent.

Turning Point
Time to Move On

The children's service board, I was appointed by the County Commissioners. This was a new experience. The welfare of children has always touched my heart. Having only one son, I always wanted a daughter. But it was not to be.

The county had a children's home for troubled children. Mostly, they were high school age. It was a good program and, in many cases, better than the homes they came from. drugs at that time (1975–1984) were not as rampant as they are today.

Parental abuse, one parent homes, and discipline were the major problems. The county had a staff of about twenty social workers. The board's job was to set policy, deal with personnel problems, and oversee the agency.

Some of the children I met at the home and reviewing the cases left me very concerned that our society was heading in the wrong direction. Foster parents were hard to find, and many questions of suitable homes for these children were an everyday problem.

The board was composed of a lawyer, housewife, a state workman, compensation employee, a service manager of a local car dealership, and me. The board worked closely with the sheriff, local police, and the courts.

To my surprise, many of the above cases were "plea-bargained" instead of going to trial. I soon learned of the *"unholy alliances" between lawyers and courts.* One case in particular caused another board member and I to go to the president and state our alarm at the plea-bargaining practices. Needless to say, the judge in question did not like our statements and called us in for a conference. We left with the explanation of how busy the courts are, etc.

We made our point that children's welfare and justice is too important, and examples should be made. However, nothing changed.

Meanwhile, I knew the sheriff personally and talked with him about the problem. He agreed that law enforcement catch the criminal and courts turn them out through the revolving door in too many cases. From that time forward, I adopted a new approach.

Several cases needed more attention. One case in particular caught my eye. A two-year-old was severely beaten. Pictures of him turned my stomach. The adult father had a history of abuse and nothing had been done to correct the problem. As per usual, charges would be filed, and here we go again. This time I intervened. The sheriff was a friend and worked closely with many in the prosecutor's office. I called him and told him he would get the case to make the arrest.

The sheriff's name was Barney, but he wasn't "Barney Fife. He had a deputy who was six feet and ten inches tall and about three hundred pounds. Barney said, "I will send L to make the arrest and will make sure the offender resists arrest." Justice served. Barney was never politically correct. He just did his job. Everyone has his rights, but everyone has his responsibilities. You reap what you sow, and this time the harvest was good. Children come first.

Micky speaking in Hawaii

Willard Scott with
my mother

CHAPTER 9

Community Involvement

My other life—family and community. My family was always first with me, although I wished I could have spent more time with them. It was the price you paid for success.

Looking back on my life, I was always involved in many things. I never learned to say, "No." I wish I had in the later years. To give you a picture of my *involvement*, here's a list as follows:

- College Scout Master
- Sunday School teacher
- Manager of varsity, basketball, football, and baseball team
- Vice president of student council
- Sports editor of *Green and White*, college newspaper
- Alpha Phi Omega Charter member and officer
- President of senior class
- Republican Party Politics—State Chairman "Students for Underwood for Governor"
- Debate team member
- *Who's Who* in American Universities and Colleges (1958)
- Selected "Tiger" by the students at Salem College "*after college*"

- Boy Scouts of America—many roles including fund-raising
- Junior achievement in high school—speaker
- American Cancer Society—fund-raising drives
- Chamber of Commerce member
- Masonic Lodge, 32 Degree—fifty-plus years as member
- Gideon International—lay speaker, chaplain, prison ministry
- Church Board member and moderator
- Zanesville, Ohio Life Underwriters Association—past president
- Lobbyist for the life insurance industries in Washington, DC
- Board member of the Temple Corp., a real estate corporation
- Franklin Local School District Board of Directors—(elected twice) past president
- Muskingum County Children's Services—board member and past president
- Motivational speaker—conducted seminars
- Southern Baptist Convention—ordained deacon
- Guardian and caretaker for the elderly
- Coach of church league basketball team
- Walked the fifty-mile trek at Philmont Boy Scout Reservation with son Alan as Eagle Scout
- Nationwide Insurance Agents Association—National President
- Travelers Rest Resort, Inc.—elected two terms to the board of directors
- Started the Veterans Memorial at Travelers Rest Resort

That old phrase, "*Let George do it,*" was about me. I just couldn't say no.

My wife's health began to decline in the early 1990s. She became diabetic and battled two different cancers. It was time to take care of her, and I did for the last ten years. Numerous operations, trips to the Cleveland Clinic, dialysis, amputations of both legs, and finally thirty-eight days in hospice by her side. She was the reason I put 110 percent into my work. Together, we traveled the country and enjoyed the fabulous president club trips. We made many new friends through air streaming (trailers and motor home) in forty-nine states and Canada. It was a full life. She beat the cancers but could not beat the diabetes. She died in 2001 at age sixty-three.

Life is not a bed of roses: Along with the good times, I have waited in the surgical waiting room thirty-one times for two wives, mother, and son.

I do not know why I have not had major health problems. I asked Margy as she was dying why it was she that had to have the health problems, and I didn't. She calmly said, "Why not me?" She was an inspiration to me for forty-three years.

I have had a blessed life—two great wives, a son, three grandchildren, and now three great grandchildren.

I hope this book will be read by my grandchildren and future great-grandchildren and will serve to motivate them to be all they can be. *That is what a happy life is all about.*

My last volunteer endeavor is at Travelers Rest Resort, our home in Florida. I was asked by Billie Doell and her husband Randy to raise $1,000 to re-landscape the front of our activity hall. This building is the center piece of the resort.

I thought about it overnight and thought wouldn't it be a great place for a United States Veteran Memorial as there are a lot of veterans in our group.

At the next Sunday night program, I asked for all volunteers who thought it was a good idea to join me to explore the possibilities. To make a long story short, over thirty responded, and the rest is history.

That was my last job as chairman, and I am very proud to close out my many undertakings with that project. We raised $47,000, not just the $1,000. Today there are over four hundred memorial bricks laid. We sold bricks to finance the memorial. I am proud to say twenty-two are there from my and Betty's family, including the medal of honor recipient, Hershel "Woody" Williams. My brick is under his—what an honor.

This was my last "Let Micky do it." It is now time for my family and this feeble attempt to write.

Looking backward, I have been busy, happy, sad, rewarded, and disappointed, but it has been a great life. I have lived before hard-topped roads, indoor plumbing, electricity, phones, central heat, and air conditioning, automobiles, radio, television, two pairs of shoes, movies, computers, power tools, washing machines, electric or gas stoves, student loans, food stamps, welfare, unemployment compensation, Pell Grants, and many other things and services that people use to provide for themselves. Individual responsibility has shifted to others, namely a do-all government. As a country, people have learned to transfer their minds and bodies. And we thought slavery was over. If it is to be, you must do it, not Uncle Sam. *We need a strong national defense, not a strong national dependency.*

We have gone from being participants to a country of spectators. This is what happened in Rome; Nero fiddled while Rome burned. The future of our country is at stake. Anarchy could happen.

Micky Graham and other volunteers raising the
flag pole on the Veterans Memorial at TR
Add flying flags!!!!!!!

Travelers Rest Veterans Memorial Flags
displaying their full glory

CHAPTER 10

Good Women Build Good Men

Women have been a major motivating force in my life. Starting with my mother and grandmother—*strong-willed* and in *control*. My grandfather was right; "find a good woman and let her be the boss." I have found that "women's intuition" is usually on target. It has been said behind every successful man, there is a strong woman. President Gerald Ford said it well: "I answer to no man and only one woman.

CEO and President of Nationwide Corporation John Fisher's rise from a starting job with Nationwide was a result of his wife motivating him. She believed in him. *It is hard to believe in yourself if your wife does not.* I have seen many agents fail because of this fact. Over the years, many women helped me to achieve.

Martha Ross—my guiding associate for twenty-three years in the insurance business. Without my wife Margy behind me, I would never have made it. I want to give credit to all of them. I had many women friends perhaps more than men friends at times. The male ego and competition sometimes clash.

Family women who guided me: my sister Mary Sue who challenged my conservative values, very successful in her own way. My aunts, each in a different way, helped me to achieve. My cousin

Jill who kept me laughing, the "Minnie Pearl" of West Virginia. Reina Mae who is the strongest woman I know.

Joan Ireland and Norma Klaiber were at my side, helping me take care of Margy in the final stages of her life. Without them, I would have had to put her in a nursing home.

Linda Sawyers—my best associate agent. She read Napoleon Hill's book *Think and Grow Rich.* She took over a large part of my business when I retired.

Wanda Mackall—a church member and client who died early "only after a good fight." We could have been brother and sister.

Billie Doell—I voted for Billie and Randy for general manager of Travelers Rest Resort when I was a board member. She was confident and feisty, and I liked that. She wasn't thirty-nine, though. I also liked Randy. Good move.

Fern Nutter—my sister-in-law (who raised two fine children and my brother-in-law, Blair)

Lola Adkins—manager Beckley exhibition coal mine

My wife Betty—a different force to deal with. She made me better and changed my life.

The women in the Bible, especially Mary and Ruth.

My granddaughter Laura, first girl in my family in over fifty years. She has become Dr. Laura. I am so proud of her.

Cheryl Graham, Alan's wife, for her character and making him happy.

All of my many girlfriends, each helped me into a maturing adult.

Ms. Gray, my high school teacher, who motivated me to get involved with Civics and gave me my first A plus in school.

Donna Jean Harvey told me I should go to college.

To the many wives who helped me motivate husbands to buy life insurance.

Brittany, Zack's wife, mother of my two great-grandchildren.

I found women to be better listeners than men were as a whole. There are exceptions of course. I found in sales, direct your attention to the wife. After all if she is not convinced, the husband won't be either.

Today, there are too many women as single parents. Men quit being men years ago, and our country is paying the price for it. Men who don't take responsibility for their family will not gain my respect, let alone their children's. I believe men should be the head of the family.

It's no wonder we have a drug epidemic of our youth. Football, hunting, fishing, and golf comes last, not first. We don't do things as a family anymore, especially eat together or pray for each other. My hat's off to women who put their family first.

CHAPTER 11

My Second Life

My new life. After Betty and I got married, I met her brother, Gene Taylor, longtime mayor of Pineville, West Virginia. To my surprise, he had that same mountain humor I had known as a boy and in the same county. When I returned to the area in 2001, I noticed a small one room church that was now closed. It had been a church that handled snakes.

I asked Gene what had happened to the church. Without hesitation, he said, "The snake died." That was Gene.

Then I fired back, 'Why don't we get a tent, a copperhead, and a rattlesnake and go around and hold revivals?" He thought it was a good money-making idea, but I would have to catch the snakes. I couldn't get ahead of him.

What happened, you may ask? Well, the snake died.

Humor transcends generations. A true story about Gene should be told: as a single man, he had a date with a blond lady with beautiful hair down to her shoulders. Unfortunately, he wrecked the car, and both were injured. The blond was bloody, and the blond hair was gone.

Gene panicked. He thought she had been scalped in the accident. The hair was a wig. Moral of the story: beware of false blonds.

Another story that proves humor goes from one generation to the another is my second grandson Zachary. He was in kindergarten and came home after the first week and informed his parents he wasn't going back; he didn't like it.

However, something changed his mind about kindergarten. *Girls.*

Alan was summoned to the school to discuss Zachary's problem. Seems he liked to pat the girls on the behind. It must be in the genes. Behavior is hereditary.

My next visit to Alan's home in Chardon, Ohio, I discussed this incident with Zachary. I said, "Zach, why did you pat the girls on the behind?"

Without a second of hesitation, he gave me a broad smile and said, "It's fun, grandpa." Case closed, the bloodline was intact.

My son, grandchildren, and great-grandchildren and spouses have been a joy to me. I am very proud of all of them.

- Alan—Eagle Scout and Ohio University graduate with honors
- Cheryl, his wife—MBA degree
- Wesley—graduate of mechanical engineering from Ohio University, very successful
- Zachary—graduate of Ohio University and MBA from Ohio State University and in real estate development
- Brittany, Zach's wife—MBA University of Ohio
- Dr. Laura—BA, BS in Miami University with masters and PhD in Math University of Kentucky
- Ralph Croyle, Laura's husband, BA Deg. in Toledo University
- Vivian, Correne, and Ruby, all under 6. My great grand-daughters. But just you wait.

Great things will happen. More to come, I hope. All of this from this old country boy who was the first in his family to graduate from college. I regret their grandmother didn't live to see the results. Perhaps she does know. She would be equally proud.

My youngest first cousin, Herbie Graham, is another Graham not satisfied with being average. He now owns the "Pinnacle" in Pineville, West Virginia. They make the best hot dogs and turkey subs anywhere. Proud of you, Herbie.

CHAPTER 12

This Is Not the End— Just the Beginning

Twilight time at eighty-four. As I come to a close in this book, I realize time is short, and I must make the most of it.

I have had a good life. I have achieved everything on my "*bucket list*," except skydiving and going up in a hot-air balloon. Both were scheduled, but illness took the front burner. I stuck to my WIN philosophy—*what is important now*.

I have been rewarded with a good family. All are well-educated and doing well. They are on their way.

Yes, *I thought and became rich* like Napoleon Hill said. I was rich in many ways, especially values. I can look in the mirror with no regrets. I did become a *millionaire* and have financed my retirement.

Discipline and good planning enabled me to retire at age sixty-two. I am proud of the over thirteen hundred life policies I wrote. Millions of dollars will come back to the Zanesville area as a result. Dreams will come true, mortgages will be paid off, better retirement income, and educations will be paid for.

To my grandchildren, great-grandchildren, and future generations, you can to it. "Think and grow rich."

No one is entitled to anything except life, freedom, and the pursuit of happiness. You came from somewhere, and you are going somewhere. Find your purpose in life, find that burning desire, and follow it. Set goals. It's up to you and no one else.

You can be optimistic or pessimistic—the choice is yours. Be happy. Dare to be different, have a *road map for your life. Don't be a door mat.*

Our country is at a crossroads. The future is on a seesaw. Too many people are satisfied with their comfort levels. *People expect entitlements rather than opportunities.* They take the easy way out.

Individual pride and accomplishment have been muted to a collective political correct value system called socialism.

As I end this book, I am reminded of a tombstone I saw out west in a boot hill in Dodge City, Kansas. It read like this:

Here Stands T. Lewis Memphis Williams
"He Did His Damndest"

Would love to know the story behind it. He wanted to be buried standing up. Must have been a proud man.

I too have tried to do my "damndest." You can too, go for it.

- I am glad I was a "poor boy."
- I was happy.
- I was privileged.
- I had opportunity.
- I had a good family.
- I had good friends.
- I had success.
- I had faith.
- I had a great life.

You can, too, go for it.

God has a place for you! Find it! Don't let your comfort zone keep you from your calling. If you don't have goals in life, you will have goofs and gaffes, and you will never know what it is to be a winner.

Follow the right POP theory. Make your life a *pursuit of purpose and not pursuit of pleasure.*

You can do it! I did! Say each morning, "If it is to be, it is up to me."

The End

SPECIAL EXPERIENCES

I have owned eleven homes and built two. I have lived in six states with extended time in several others. I have moved twenty-nine times.

Places I have lived:

West Virginia

- Clear Fork
- Welch
- Glover
- Wyoming
- Dorothy
- Beckley
- Hinton
- Daniels
- Salem
- Clarksburg
- Leewood
- Acme
- Ronda
- Rainelle

Florida

- Polk City
- Dade City

Ohio

- Zanesville
- Columbus

Texas

- Highlands

Virginia

- Narrows

New Jersey

- Mendham

The top twenty-five girlfriends before marriage who helped me have a full and interesting life:

1. *Patty*. First girlfriend, very pretty
2. *Lorraine*. Good friend
3. *Betty*. High school "crush," second wife fifty-two years latter
4. *Margie*. She never gave me a chance
5. *Carol*. My movie partner
6. *Billie* C. Junior prom date—could have been
7. *Suzanne*. President senior class, prom date
8. *Chessie*. Steady for a long time, "escaped" lucky
9. *Normadean*. Mysterious, pretty, a fast driver
10. *Wava*. Blond, pretty, a steady girlfriend before college nice girl, could have been the one
11. *Hannah*. The other high school crush—married someone else
12. *Mary E*. College friend—not ready to settle down
13. *Nola*. Scared me—wanted to get married

14. *Billy Z.* Beautiful little "china doll," I was too dumb
15. *Dorothy.* Nothing but class
16. *Betty T.* Long-distance romance
17. *Laura.* Good buddy
18. *Elizabeth.* Farm girl—her mom fed me
19. *Becky.* I liked her, a definite contender
20. *Lea.* Good prankster buddy
21. *Patty H.* Too far away, rich family, tempting
22. *Sue.* Amazing girl with a handicap
23. *Sharon.* Time passed us by
24. *Patty T.* Blond—liked another boy better
25. *Margaret (Margy) Nutter.* My wife, my right arm for forty-three years.

Betty and I will soon be married seventeen years. We decided to get married over the phone sight unseen. I am a closer. Scored two homeruns with wives. I will never go to the plate again. Retire with a 1,000 percent batting average.

Cars I have owned. Girls and cars were my two main interests outside of goals and service.

My good friend, Cecil Harper, educated me about cars. Cecil owns Harpers Auto Body in Zanesville, Ohio.

1. 1937 Chevrolet truck
2. 1950 Chevrolet truck
3. 1948 Nash Ambassador
4. 1949 Dodge roadster convertible
5. 1946 Chrysler Saratoga
6. 1952 Plymouth Belvedere
7. 1958 Hillman sedan
8. 1959 Hillman station wagon
9. 1952 Chevrolet sedan
10. 1947 Chrysler Windsor
11. 1951 Chrysler Imperial
12. 1941 Buick Special
13. 1964 Corvair convertible

14. 1961 GMC Caballero
15. 1971 Mercury Grand Marquis
16. 1970 Mercury Cougar
17. 1960 Plymouth Valiant
18. 1984 Chevrolet Van
19. 1985 Ford Ranger
20. 1973 Mercury Grand Marquis
21. 1968 Cadillac Sedan Deville
22. 1986 Cadillac Sedan Deville
23. 1990 Cadillac Fleetwood 60 Special
24. 1955 Ford Fairlane
25. 1985 Mercury Grand Marquis
26. 1979 Dodge Omni
27. 1972 Lincoln Town Car
28. 1975 Oldsmobile Cutlass
29. 1968 Buick Electra
30. 1965 Buick Special
31. 1967 V.W. Bug
32. 1968 Chevrolet truck
33. 1992 Lincoln Town Car
34. 1999 Subaru Legacy
35. 1998 Subaru SW
36. 1995 Lincoln Town Car
37. 1979 Dodge Van
38. 1929 Shay model A (my pride and joy)
39. 1999 Ford Van
40. 2010 Lincoln MKT
41. 2011 Ford Flex
42. 2006 Jaguar convertible
43. 1973 Mercedes 450
44. 2014 Ford Explorer
45. 2015 Chrysler 300 C
46. 2015 Ford Escape
47. 1937 Packard replica
48. 1986 Dodge Van
49. 2005 GMC Denali

50. 2006 Oldsmobile Alero
51. 2006 Dodge Ram pickup
52. 2014 Lincoln MKT

My next car—necessity is the mother of invention.

New company—stock still available.

Two-seaters available on request. Take your favorite seat with you.

No stopping or waiting. Patent depending.

There are several more that I cannot remember. Cars and girls were my hobbies, both expensive.

Enjoying white water rafting in the Double "Z," New River in West Virginia

Some of my cars

1929 Model "A" Shay Ford Roadster

1937 Packard replica

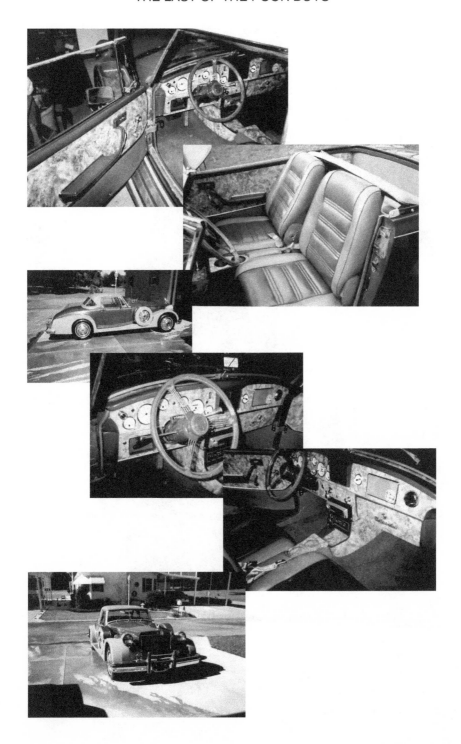

1947 Chrysler Windsor (five-passenger coupe)

Here is a list of some of the jobs I have had:

- The company store
- Truck driver
- Butcher; meat cutter
- Laborer—right of way, farm work

- Gas station—gas, oil, and grease autos
- Haddad and Caputo—wholesale produce laborer and sales
- Mopped and cleaned restaurants for meals
- Washed dishes for meals at the college cafeteria
- Sold the Grit newspaper
- Newspaper boy at the Charleston Daily Mail
- Camp Director at Boy Scouts of America
- Sold books
- Mowed yards (no power mowers then)
- Hoed corn (raised vegetables to sell)
- The A&P Co. coproduce clerk
- Boy Scouts of America district executive
- Reporter at the Times Recorder Newspaper on weekends
- Building materials salesman
- School teacher—high school English and history
- Kroger company—managed three stores
- Owner of country carry/out, Quick Stop Shop
- Partner, wrecker, airbag recovery
- Night-Crawlers sales in college
- One day in the coal mines
- New York Life agent
- IDS Agent for six years
- Micky Graham and Associates—twenty-four years of insurance and financial services
- Motivational speaker
- Odd jobs in college
- Painting
- Cleaning

ABOUT THE AUTHOR

Academic Background

- Graduate of East Bank High School, class of 1952
- Graduate of Salem College 1958 BA degree
- Listed in *Who's Who* in American universities and colleges
- President of senior class
- Ohio University, graduate work
- Graduate Success Motivation Institute 1961
- American college, CLU, CHFC, LUTCF designations
- Lifelong study at the University of "Hard Knocks"
- Listed in *Who's Who* of outstanding Americans

Author's Literary Attempts

Micky Graham has written many articles and stories that have been published. Many of these were connected to the insurance and financial planning career that spanned thirty years. He started his journalistic endeavors with the *Charleston Daily Mail* (delivering papers). Among his writing experiences—a reporter for the *Times Recorder* of Zanesville, Ohio. Sports editor for the *Green and White*, a student newspaper at

Salem College (now Salem International University), and contributor to the Outhouse Gazette.

Among the author's literary attempts:

From Corncobs to Charming, a story of a poor boy who moved to the city of Zanesville's Ohio.

Why I Left West Virginia, a story of a Republican climbing out of the toilet" 1959 vintage.

Archie and Me, a story of an ideal father in law son-in-law relationship, a true story

Surviving Shopping in Marriage a how-to book for all the husband's and Hillary Clinton.

Let George Do It describing the welfare system and are decaying morals.

Baptizing the Cats a true-life experience.